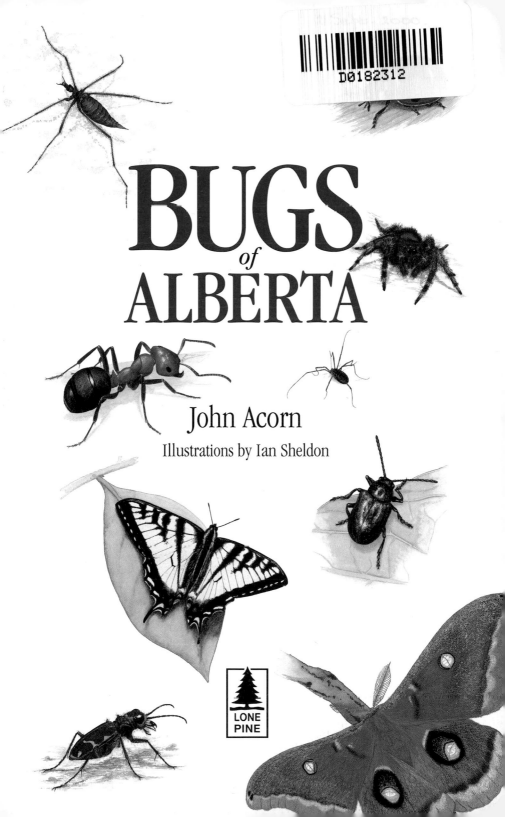

BUGS
of
ALBERTA

John Acorn

Illustrations by Ian Sheldon

LONE
PINE

© 2000 by Lone Pine Publishing
First printed in 2000   10 9 8 7 6 5 4 3 2 1
Printed in Canada

The Publisher: Lone Pine Publishing

10145 - 81 Ave.	1901 Raymond Ave. SW, Suite C
Edmonton, AB T6E 1W9	Renton, WA 98055
Canada	USA

Website: http://www.lonepinepublishing.com

Canadian Cataloguing in Publication Data
Acorn, John Harrison, 1958–
  Bugs of Alberta

  Includes bibliographical references and index.
  ISBN 1-55105-146-X

  1. Insects—Alberta—Identification. I. Title.
QL476.A36 2000   595.7'097123   C00-910507-7

Editorial Director: Nancy Foulds
Project Editor: Lee Craig
Production Manager: Jody Reekie
Design, Layout & Production: Heather Markham
Book & Cover Design: Robert Weidemann
Cover Illustration: Ian Sheldon
Illustrations: Ian Sheldon
Technical Review: Rob Cannings
Separations & Film: Elite Lithographers Co.

The following illustrations are used with permission from Ian Sheldon © 1999: pp. 26–28; pp. 31–35; pp. 37–39; pp. 41–55.

We acknowledge the financial support of the Government of Canada through the Book Publishing Industry Development Program (BPIDP) for our publishing activities.

PC: P4

CONTENTS

DEDICATION

To John and Bert Carr, whose love of our native beetles has been an inspiration to many a budding Alberta "bugster."

ACKNOWLEDGEMENTS

As much as I enjoyed writing this book, I enjoyed working with Ian Sheldon even more. As each of his illustrations appeared, I became more and more excited about the project, and I can't thank Ian enough for his dedication to both the art and science of "bugs." As well, the book would not have been possible without the characteristic generosity of many entomologists and arachnologists. Special thanks go to Felix Sperling, George Ball and Danny Shpeley of the University of Alberta's E.H. Strickland Entomological Museum, for allowing access to specimens and records and for freely sharing their vast expertise. I would also like to thank the following people for reviewing text and graciously responding to queries: Gary Anweiler, Brian Brown, Rob Cannings, Ed Fuller, Robert Holmberg, Reuben Kaufman, Dave Lawrie, David Maddison, Chris Schmidt, Ales Smetana, Terry Thormin and Daryl Williams. The staff of Lone Pine Publishing have been a pleasure to work with, and I would especially like to recognize Lee Craig, Nancy Foulds and Shane Kennedy for their contributions. Finally, I would like to thank Dena Stockburger for her loving support, Jesse Acorn for his three-year-old perspective on life, my parents for allowing me to be a bugster throughout my childhood and all the enthusiastic folks who make up the Alberta Lepidopterists' Guild, the "Hyperboreal Odonatists' Guild and Social Club" and the "Voyagers to the Vortek."

European Skipper
p. 26

Canadian Tiger
Swallowtail, p. 27

Cabbage White
p. 28

Clouded Sulphur
p. 29

BUTTERFLIES

Spring Azure
p. 30

Purplish Copper
p. 31

Meadow Fritillary
p. 32

Great Spangled
Fritillary, p. 33

White Admiral
p. 34

Pearl Crescent
p. 35

Mourning Cloak
p. 36

Painted Lady
p. 37

Red Admiral
p. 38

Common Wood
Nymph, p. 39

Monarch
p. 40

Polyphemus
Moth, p. 41

MOTHS

Columbian Silk
Moth, p. 42

One-Eyed
Sphinx, p. 43

Big Poplar
Sphinx, p. 44

Snowberry
Clearwing, p. 45

Galium Sphinx
p. 46

Garden Tiger
Moth, p. 47

Spotted Tussock
Moth, p. 48

Police Car
Moth, p. 49

Virginia Ctenucha
p. 50

MOTHS

Forest Tent Caterpillar
Moth, p. 51

Black Witch
p. 52

White Underwing
p. 53

Once-Married
Underwing, p. 54

Pale Beauty
p. 55

Claybank Tiger
Beetle, p. 56

Purple-Rimmed
Carabus, p. 57

Fiery Hunter
p. 58

Sidewalk Carabid
p. 59

BEETLES

Stag-Jawed
Carabid, p. 60

Burying Beetle
p. 61

Hairy Rove Beetle
p. 62

May Beetle
p. 63

Ten-Lined June
Beetle, p. 64

Gold Dust
Buprestid, p. 65

Resplendant Click
Beetle, p. 66

Sapphire-Winged
Click Beetle, p. 67

Beer Beetle
p. 68

Stink Beetle
p. 69

Nuttall's Blister
Beetle, p. 70

Seven-Spot
Ladybug, p. 71

Two-Spot Ladybug
p.72

Thirteen-Spot
Ladybug, p. 73

Spruce Sawyer
p. 74

Dogbane Beetle
p. 75

Golden Tortoise
Beetle, p. 76

Strawberry Root
Weevil, p. 77

Wood Ant
p. 78

Carpenter Ant
p. 79

ANTS, WASPS & ALLIES

Nevada Bumblebee
p. 80

Blue Horntail
p. 81

Bald-Faced Hornet
p. 82

Yellow Jacket
p. 83

Paper Wasp
p. 84

Stump Stabber
p. 85

Thread-Waisted
Wasp, p. 86

Spider Wasp
p. 87

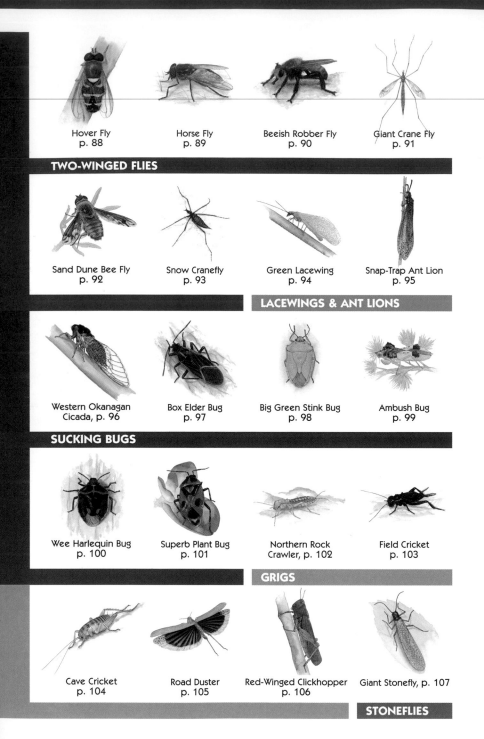

Hover Fly
p. 88

Horse Fly
p. 89

Beeish Robber Fly
p. 90

Giant Crane Fly
p. 91

TWO-WINGED FLIES

Sand Dune Bee Fly
p. 92

Snow Cranefly
p. 93

Green Lacewing
p. 94

Snap-Trap Ant Lion
p. 95

LACEWINGS & ANT LIONS

Western Okanagan
Cicada, p. 96

Box Elder Bug
p. 97

Big Green Stink Bug
p. 98

Ambush Bug
p. 99

SUCKING BUGS

Wee Harlequin Bug
p. 100

Superb Plant Bug
p. 101

Northern Rock
Crawler, p. 102

Field Cricket
p. 103

GRIGS

Cave Cricket
p. 104

Road Duster
p. 105

Red-Winged Clickhopper
p. 106

Giant Stonefly, p. 107

STONEFLIES

German Cockroach
p. 108

Boreal Bluet
p. 109

Taiga Bluet
p. 110

Common Spreadwing
p. 111

COCKROACHES

DRAGONFLIES & DAMSELFLIES

Variable Darner
p. 112

Pale Snaketail
p. 113

American Emerald
p. 114

Hudsonian Whiteface
p. 115

Four-Spotted
Skimmer, p. 116

Cherry-Faced Meadowhawk
p. 117

Black Meadowhawk
p. 118

Snow Flea
p. 119

SPRINGTAILS

Kayak Pond
Skater, p. 120

Giant Water
Bug, p. 121

Auden's Water
Boatman, p. 122

Common
Backswimmer, p. 123

Acilius Diving
Beetle, p. 124

AQUATIC INSECTS

Mid-Sized Diving
Beetle, p. 125

Giant Diving
Beetle, p. 126

Whirligig Beetle
p. 127

Obtuse Water
Scavenger Beetle, p. 128

Damselfly Larva
p. 129

AQUATIC LARVAE

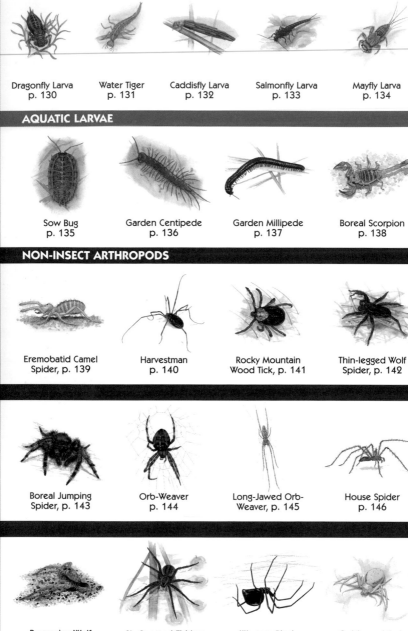

Dragonfly Larva
p. 130

Water Tiger
p. 131

Caddisfly Larva
p. 132

Salmonfly Larva
p. 133

Mayfly Larva
p. 134

AQUATIC LARVAE

Sow Bug
p. 135

Garden Centipede
p. 136

Garden Millipede
p. 137

Boreal Scorpion
p. 138

NON-INSECT ARTHROPODS

Eremobatid Camel
Spider, p. 139

Harvestman
p. 140

Rocky Mountain
Wood Tick, p. 141

Thin-legged Wolf
Spider, p. 142

Boreal Jumping
Spider, p. 143

Orb-Weaver
p. 144

Long-Jawed Orb-
Weaver, p. 145

House Spider
p. 146

Burrowing Wolf
Spider, p. 147

Six-Spotted Fishing
Spider, p. 148

Western Black
Widow, p. 149

Goldenrod Crab
Spider, p. 150

INTRODUCTION

This book is one for bugsters. If you haven't heard the term, don't feel left out. I think I invented it, with the help of my friends. We needed a word for people who are fascinated by insects and enjoy them for no other reason than their intrinsic niftiness. "Amateur entomologist" seemed too stuffy, as did "insect enthusiast" and "entomophile." "Bugger" is out of the question. So are "bug-nut" and "bug-lover," mostly because they sound too silly. I did find the term "entomaniac" popular among some of the people I know, but it probably isn't the best one to use as a recruiting tool. Maniacs are crazy, but we bugsters are merely enthusiastic.

Even the word "bug" is fraught with problems. In the strict language of entomology, a bug is a member of the Order Hemiptera, often pedantically called "true bugs," although I prefer the more neutral "sucking bugs" myself. All other insects, including true bugs, are simply "insects." In technical language, when one expands the taxonomic scope to include spiders, centipedes and millipedes, one has to resort to the phrase "terrestrial arthropods" (see p. 18). It's tough to say that without sounding pretentious. So let's just cut through all of this confusion, and call the critters "bugs," and the people who love them "bugsters." It works for me. The only reason these terms were difficult to decide on is that our language simply hasn't been called upon to develop everyday words to go with these ideas.

DID YOU KNOW? ... Alberta has about 20,000 species of bugs? Really!

PAINTED LADY

Given the enduring appeal of bugs, it is odd that the language hasn't advanced more. Some bugs, like butterflies, are beautiful. Others, like ladybugs and bumblebees, are familiar personalities in the garden. Then there are those bugs that are fascinating in a scary sort of way, such as spiders and scorpions. A wonderful diversity of insect life exists here in Alberta, and a great deal of delight is generated by such a wide variety of living forms "right under our noses." Biologists these days like to call this wide variety "biodiversity," and some people claim that humans are naturally pre-disposed to appreciate and crave contact with it. This idea, in turn, is called "biophilia," which can be translated as "the love of living things." I am not so sure that I agree with the biophilia hypothesis, because there are so many people out there who couldn't care less about the world of plants and animals. For those people who feel the connection, however, the idea of bio-philia can be a great comfort.

Of course, our society has developed a rather disdainful attitude toward bugs. To some people, because not all bugs are beneficial to humans and every single bug is smaller than a hamster, these creatures have little importance. As a consequence, most of the people who have done things to improve our understanding and appreciation of bugs have been professional biologists. Of these, entomologists study insects, while arachnologists study arachnids. Those scientists who study other sorts of bugs are generally called "inverte-brate zoologists," and this term can also be used to refer to the whole gang at once. Here in Alberta, the tradition of bug study has gone on primarily in the universities, as well as in research facilities operated by both the provincial and federal governments. Forest and crop pests have attracted their share of attention, and so have biting flies and other bugs of medical or veterinary importance. Yet some professional bugsters have studied their subjects out of pure fascination, and many talented and devoted amateurs have contributed to the knowledge of Alberta's bugs as well.

We seem poised for a resurgence of interest in our arthropod neighbours, what with the proliferation of bug-related movies, children's books and toys in the last few years. I suppose this book will probably be considered part of the same "craze," but I also hope it will survive beyond that. For this reason, I have tried to make this book as entomologically correct as I could, while still retaining a spirit of fun and informality. Having watched Alberta go through the dinosaur craze of the 1980s, it seems to me that after the wave has passed, we will still be left with an interesting subject. As well, the interesting things about it will still be generated by the core group of people who cared before the fad, and who will continue to care in the future.

Alberta has about 20,000 species of bugs. This number is a guess, of course. The reason we don't know exactly is that new species are still waiting to be discovered by science, and many species that are known elsewhere are waiting to be found here in Alberta. Choosing the 125 "coolest" species was a challenge for me. I tried to pick bugs that are

1) **big**
2) **colourful**
3) **really hard to miss or**
4) **extremely weird.**

The point of this book is to introduce you to the bugs of Alberta, not to serve as a guide to the whole shebang. I hope you realize that to a hard-core bugster like myself, every single one of those 20,000 species has the potential to be wonderfully interesting. In other words, this book is supposed to be more inspiring than scholastic.

It is traditional in a book of this sort to divide the province into biophysical regions, and discuss the overall topography and vegetation of Alberta. I am going to quickly skip over this task, because most of the insects I am about to discuss are widely distributed and not tied to any particular part of the province. The exceptions come mainly from the southeast corner, where the land is flat and the trees grow only in the valleys of the major rivers. These parts of the province are called the grasslands, or the prairies.

Alberta is shaped like a tall semi-rectangle (narrower at the top than the bottom), with a "bite" out of the southwest corner. This bite is the line of the Continental

HARVESTMAN

13

Divide, and along it we find the Rocky Mountains. Over much of its northern third, boreal forests, made up mostly of poplars and spruce, cover the province. Between the boreal forests and the prairies, a band of parkland exists, in which most of the trees are aspen poplars and meadows are common, too. Obvious exceptions to this pattern include the warm, grassland-ish Peace River district of the northwest and the high, cool, mountain-like Cypress Hills in the southeast. Of course, this overall pattern has been strongly obscured by agriculture and forestry, as well as changes in climate, but for those readers who want a thumbnail introduction to the place, this description is Alberta in a biological nutshell.

BASIC BUG BANTER

Like any science, the study of bugs has its own jargon. Some of its words have plain-language equivalents, but others do not. Unavoidably then, it is important to get the gist of things before going on to read more about the bugs themselves. I suppose I could have presented this section as a glossary, but I think it will be more interesting as a sort of condensed textbook. I hope you agree.

Bug Structure

Let's start with the structure, or anatomy, of bugs, and let's also start at the front end of an average specimen. They all have a head, and on the head there are almost always eyes (with either one lens or many), a mouth, a set of appendages called **mouthparts** and a pair of feelers called **antennae** (one is an antenna). Eyes with multiple lenses are called **compound eyes**; eyes with one lens are called **ocelli** (singularly, an ocellus).

On many bugs the head is joined to the rest of the body by an obvious line or groove, and it is somewhat moveable on a flexible but very short neck. In others (spiders and scorpions, for example), the head is part-and-parcel of a larger body part—the **cephalothorax**—that also bears the legs. Major body parts, which is to say the head, thorax, cephalothorax or abdomen, are often further divided into segments, and the segments may or may not be easy to recognize on the surface.

Insects have a separate **thorax**, which is easy to recognize because it is the part of the body that bears the legs. The thorax is, in turn, divided into three segments, each of which bears a single pair of legs. If wings are present, they are borne by the middle and hind segments of the thorax. In many groups, the front wings are thickened and serve as wing covers for the hindwings. The three segments that make up the thorax are called the **prothorax, mesothorax** and **metathorax**. The top of the prothorax is called the **pronotum**, and on beetles no other parts of the thorax are visible from above, except the wing covers.

Everything past the thorax is called the **abdomen**. At the tip of the abdomen, one finds the anus, the reproductive structures, and in many types of bugs, a rear-facing set of "feelers" called **cerci** (singularly, a cercus).

A few other obvious aspects of the anatomy of a bug include **spiracles** on the sides of the thorax and abdomen (openings for the multi-branched breathing tubes of insects, called the **tracheal system**) or book lung openings on the underside of spiders, near the silk-producing **spinnerets**. Some aquatic insects (insects that live in the water) have **gills** as well, most of which are leafy or finely branched projections from the body. Scorpions have comb-like sensory appendages called **pectines** on the underside of their cephalothorax.

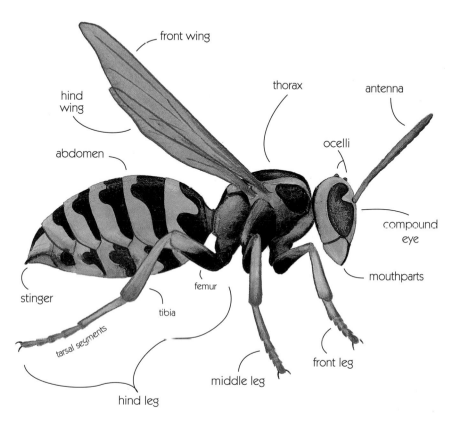

front wing

hind wing

thorax

antenna

abdomen

ocelli

compound eye

mouthparts

stinger

femur

tibia

tarsal segments

front leg

middle leg

hind leg

Life History

Now let's discuss life history. Most bugs begin life as an egg. The egg then hatches into a baby bug, but not all baby bugs look like their parents. Generally, if the young that hatch from the eggs look more or less like the adults (baby grasshoppers, for example), they are likely to be called **nymphs**. If the young are clearly different from the adults, the word **larva** is more widely used (although the larvae of butterflies and moths are called **caterpillars**). Some aquatic nymphs are called naiads, and spider babies are simply spiderlings. Entomologists have recently agreed to use the word "larvae" to refer to all sorts of immature insects, but they have to fight a long history of confusion to do so. If you think this situation is complicated, compare it to the difficulty with mammals, where you have to distinguish among pups, kids, calves, kits, foals, colts, lambs and so on.

As bugs grow, they have to shed their outer covering, which is called the **exoskeleton** (or more properly, the exocuticle), numerous times. Some bugs simply increase in size until they are large enough and mature enough to reproduce. Others show more obvious changes as they grow, the most common of which is the development of wings and genitalia. The genitalia are the sexual parts of bugs, and they are often complicated, involving claspers, levers, pliers, syringes and the like. Sometimes, they are visible from the outside, and sometimes not. In spiders, one pair of mouthparts serves as the male sex organs (the palps), and in dragonflies and damselflies the males have one set of genitalia at the tip of the abdomen and another at the base. The base of a structure, by the way, is always the place where the structure attaches to the rest of the body.

When a bug reaches the full-grown, ready-to-reproduce state, it is simply called an **adult**. However, in order for caterpillars and other grub-like larvae to become adults, they first have to enter into a resting stage, called the **pupa** (the plural is pupae), during which an amazing transformation takes place. Butterfly pupae are sometimes called chrysalids. Remember that the silk covering that some caterpillars make when they pupate, and not the pupa itself, is called a **cocoon**.

The change from young to adult is called **metamorphosis**, and there are three sorts: If the change is gradual, what we have is **gradual metamorphosis**; if it involves the development of wings, or some other fairly major change in body form, it is called **incomplete metamorphosis**; and if it involves a pupa stage, it is called **complete metamorphosis**. These terms are old-fashioned and, of course, nothing is defective about an insect with **incomplete** metamorphosis.

THE AUTHOR, BUG-WATCHING WITH HIS SON JESSE   PHOTO: DENA STOCKBURGER

Ecology

The ecology of bugs depends on how they interact with other living things and with their non-living environment. The place where an insect lives is called its **habitat**, a word that means about the same as environment. All of the plants and animals in a given habitat are called a **community**, and larger such groupings are called **ccosystems**. An insect may recognize its habitat by soil type, by slope (or flatness), by altitude, by water characteristics (flow speed, dissolved oxygen, temperature and so on) or by the presence of specific types of prey or species of plants. If an insect eats plants, the plants are called **host plants** or **food plants**, and the insects are called **herbivores**. If an insect drinks nectar, the plants are called **nectar plants**. Insects that eat other creatures are **predators**, while the creatures they eat are **prey**. If an insect lives on or inside a host animal, and either kills it very slowly or not at all, it is called a **parasite**. If it eventually kills the host and is a parasite only in the larval stage, it is called a **parasitoid**. If an insect eats things that are already dead, it is called a **scavenger**. If it eats poop, it is said to be **coprophagous**. Complex, isn't it?

17

Bug Systematics

Systematics is the study of how living things are related, in an evolutionary sense. To reconstruct the evolutionary tree of life, you really have to start with the basic unit of evolutionary change, the species. Species are groups of living things that can interbreed in nature without hybridizing ("crossing") with other species—at least not *too* much. Species are grouped with other closely related species into genera, the singular of which is genus. Genera are grouped into families, families into orders, orders into classes and classes into phyla. This system is called the Linnaean system of classification. The singular of phyla is phylum, and all of the critters in this book belong to one phylum, the Arthropoda or "joint-legged animals." These are what I call "bugs."

Within the Phylum Arthropoda, I have chosen examples from five classes: the crustaceans (Class Crustacea), the millipedes (Class Diplopoda), the centipedes (Class Chilopoda), the arachnids (Class Arachnida) and the insects (Class Insecta). The arachnids are further divided into five orders in this book: the spiders (Order Aranaea), the harvestmen (Order Opiliones), the scorpions (Order Scorpionida), the camel spiders (Order Solifugae) and the mites and ticks (Order Acarina).

Because of their great diversity, the situation with the insects is a bit more complex. Beginning with the flightless insects, we start with springtails, in the Order Collembola. Springtails show gradual metamorphosis. Then we come to the insects with wings and incomplete metamorphosis, beginning with the dragonflies and damselflies in the Order Odonata, the mayflies in the Order Ephemeroptera and the stoneflies in the Order Plecoptera. Next come the grasshoppers, crickets and such (the "grigs," as some people call them) in the Order Orthoptera and the cockroaches in the Order Dictyoptera. Sucking bugs (the so-called "true" bugs) also fall into this part of the classification, and they form the Order Hemiptera.

The rest of the insects have complete metamorphosis, with a pupa stage: the two-winged flies (the "true" flies) in the Order Diptera; the wasps, bees and ants in the Order Hymenoptera; the beetles in the Order Coleoptera; the caddisflies in the Order Trichoptera; the lacewings and ant-lions in the Order Neuroptera; and the butterflies and moths in the Order Lepidoptera.

By the way, "ptera" means wing, Hemiptera means half-wing, Diptera means two-wing, Lepidoptera means scaly-wing and so on. If you look into the meanings of scientific names, it will help you remember them, but there is no substitute for simply memorizing the words and getting on with the more interesting aspects of entomology. Note as well that one species is abbreviated as "sp." and many species as "spp."

In most bug books, the various groups are presented in the order that I have just given. This order places closely related groups together, and it begins with those bugs that are most primitive (in the sense of resembling the long-extinct common ancestor of the entire group) and ends with those bugs that are most derived (a term that means they have undergone a great deal of evolutionary change). In this book, however, I have chosen to reverse the order. My order still keeps related species together and gives you all the insight that the traditional order does, but it also allows you to start with butterflies and moths, rather than springtails. My goal is to get you to like these animals, so I have chosen to begin with the niftiest ones. At the end of the insects, however, I have "artificially" grouped a number of unrelated aquatic insects together in one section, because that is the way many entomologists think of them—as a unit. The non-insects follow the aquatic insects.

BEING A BUGSTER

This book is not about pests and how to kill them. Sure, some bugs are harmful, and I don't object to fighting back when the need arises, so long as no other species, or people, are caught in the crossfire. In fact, you'll find that some of my favourite bugs are pests. After all, it is always possible to admire the positive qualities of your enemies, even in the heat of battle.

Most bugs, however, are harmless, and all good bugsters know that they are the very backbone of the ecology of Alberta, responsible for everything from pollination to decomposition, soil formation, regulation of other bugs and "weeds," food for birds and mammals and so on. Without apology, I think that all bugs are worthy of admiration and respect, and at least a passing glance. If you don't understand bugs, you really don't understand the world in which you live.

Bugs are easy to find, at least on warm days during bug season, which means roughly late March through October. Bugs are only hard to find for four months of the year, which in my opinion is pretty darn good. Of course, May through September is the best time for bugs, during which they are downright hard to miss. Bugs live in almost every conceivable habitat, from the alpine tundra on the tops of the highest mountains to the driest prairie sand dune, the insides of caves, the insides of our homes and every place in between.

SHALLOW LAKES TEEM WITH AQUATIC INSECTS AND STRANDED LADYBUGS   PHOTO: DENA STOCKBURGER

Still, if you want to go out searching for bugs, I suggest looking for them in such habitats as

1) under rocks and boards (and remember to put the rocks and boards back once you look)

2) on plants, and especially on flowers and the undersides of leaves

3) at lights at night (but not the yellow bug-free lights)

4) in the water, especially where there are lots of water plants

5) on bare, sandy ground, even if it is far from water

6) at various sorts of "bait."

My favourite bug baits include various mixtures of beer and sugar, painted on trees for moths and butterflies, as well as less appealing things such as dung and carrion. Don't feel bad if you choose to ignore the bug-baiting option—after all, many sorts of bait are downright unhygienic. Remember not to touch the bait, and always wash your hands afterwards—something my mother used to tell me often when I was a junior bugster.

In general, bugs like warm weather more than cool, and they are easier to find in sunny places than in the shade. They prefer humid days to dry, but they don't do much in the rain. Warm nights will bring out many flying insects, such as moths, while cool ones will not. During a full moon, bugs are less attracted to lights. Wind does not necessarily deter bug activity, but it certainly makes the bugs harder to find and to follow. Daytime bugs get going at about 9 a.m., and they slow down appreciably by around 7 p.m., at least during mid-summer.

The easiest way to get a close look at a bug is to catch it, examine it, and let it go. Nets are easy to make, and good ones are also inexpensive to buy through mail-order. Small bugs can be placed in clean jars for a brief period, while large ones, such as butterflies and dragonflies, can be gently examined while still in the net. Many bugs can gently be handled. In my opinion, this last method is the overall best way to approach the study of bugs, and it gives a great deal of satisfaction for very little effort. All of the suggestions that follow involve more work and more of a commitment to mastering unusual techniques.

If you want to watch bugs without disturbing them, you can do it the old-fashioned way, on your elbows with a Sherlock Holmes magnifying glass, or you can try other sorts of optical tools. I can recommend the Bushnell close-focusing 8-power monocular, model 14-8200 (it focuses to a distance of about 20 cm, and it costs less than $50). You might also try a pair of compact binoculars, such as the Bushnell Natureview 8X30, with a Nikon 5T close-up lens held in front of them (total cost between $200 to $250). These binoculars give you a clear view of the bug, at a distance of about half a metre, with both eyes at once.

Depending on what sort of bug you choose to watch, your style will have to be modified. When I watch tiger beetles, I find myself crawling around on the sand, continually moving to follow my subjects. On the other hand, I often place a small folding chair in front of a buggy-looking plant, and then sit in one place while scanning the flowers, leaves and stems for interesting creatures on which to spy.

Bug watching can teach us a great deal. Because the behaviour of many of our local bugs is poorly known, any of us has the ability to make useful observations once we have learned to identify the creatures we are encountering. As well, simply immersing yourself in the lives of insects and other buggy critters is a wonderful way to make a deep and moving connection with the non-human world all around us. You can be as scientific or as recreational as you want.

If you make detailed observations of particular sorts of insect, it is probably a good idea to collect a few "voucher specimens," so other bugsters can confirm your identifications after the fact (for really easy identifications, a close-up photograph will also suffice). When I was young, the only way to approach bug study was to make a collection. Collecting is still allowed, almost anywhere, except in national and provincial parks, but it is no longer a popular activity.

If you choose to make a collection for educational or scientific reasons, remember to limit your catch, treat every specimen with respect, take the time to label, arrange and store the specimens correctly, and plan to donate them to a university or museum once you are done with them. Instructions for insect collecting are easy to come by, and for the most part you will only encounter ill-will when you collect butterflies and moths—most people feel little sympathy for other sorts of bugs.

Increasingly, however, bugsters are polarizing into collecting and anti-collecting camps. I wish they weren't, but because they are, I want to briefly discuss the matter. Collectors claim they do not harm bug populations—bugs generally have short generation times and high reproduction rates, and recover from "harvest" much more easily than vertebrates. Collectors also point out that the identities of pinned specimens can be confirmed, whereas sightings are always subject to doubt. Anti-collectors, on the other hand, are reluctant to admit that collecting is always innocent, because it *must* be possible for a large enough group of collectors to cause local extinctions of small isolated "colonies" of rare bugs. These rare bugs are exactly the sorts of bugs that collectors seek, so this fear could be well-founded if collecting were ever to become truly popular (which in itself seems unlikely). Unfortunately, these isolated populations also become places where collectors and anti-collectors come into uncomfortable proximity with one another. At this point, it is very difficult for the watchers to do their thing with collectors chasing the very bugs they want to observe and *vice versa*.

When I try my hardest to be rational about this subject, it seems obvious to me that insect collectors are not a big threat to the insects of Alberta. In fact, I believe they are inconsequential. Pesticides, introduced species and habitat destruction are all of much greater concern. It seems to me that the real core of the collector/anti-collector debate has to do with two rather unscientific human motives. First, no one likes having their freedom (or the freedom of their favourite bugs) restricted. Second, collectors and anti-collectors seem to dislike the sorts of people that each other represents. On the one hand, let's admit that it is difficult to sympathize with those people who kill the very objects of their passion. On the other, it is difficult to take a person's scientific motives seriously when he or she is willfully unsure of the identities of the creatures he or she is observing and could

INSECT PHOTOGRAPHY CAN BE AS SIMPLE OR AS COMPLEX AS YOU LIKE   PHOTO: MARISSA SHOEMAKER

easily remedy the situation by catching a few. It also seems clear to me that peer pressure has a great deal to do with the attitudes of individual bug-sters—in a group of watchers, no one dares bring out a net; among collectors, the binoculars stay in their cases.

As for my personal approach, I usually go out with nothing but binoculars and a camera, content to watch and admire. When I'm doing something scientific, I also take a net. I sometimes collect a specimen or two, but most of the time I use institutional collections for research. I still find many uses for pinned insects (for example, when writing this book), but I no longer feel a deep-seated need to possess them for myself. I try to act respectfully toward bugs whenever I can, but I'll admit that it is difficult to avoid inconsistency—swatting mosquitoes or splattering bugs on a windshield one moment, then treating bugs like endangered panda bears the

23

next. The way I see it, this sort of "hypocrisy" is inescapable, and one can use it to either justify a callous attitude toward bugs, or accept it and atone by acting kindly toward them whenever possible.

Another fascinating activity is insect rearing, which is much less controversial than collecting or watching, because people who rear bugs are more-or-less forced to treat them with loving care, and they will inevitably acquire a specimen or two through accidental mortality. Most often, when people want to rear bugs, they start with some caterpillars and wait and see what type of butterfly or moth they will turn into. To rear caterpillars, put them in a well-ventilated cage and provide them with plenty of leaves to eat. Place the cut stems in water with some means of preventing the caterpillars from drowning in the water supply (I place soft foam around the stems). When they are ready, some caterpillars pupate above ground, but for those that dig into the soil, make sure they have some potting soil or peat to dig in when the time comes. For those species that hibernate as pupae, place the pupae in the refrigerator for the winter, and mist them with water if they become dry—refrigerators are terribly dry places. Rearing caterpillars is not easy; as they grow they require more and more fresh food, and their quarters need to be cleaned frequently. If you have a lot of them, they can be almost as much effort as a new puppy!

For other insects, you will have to be more creative with your rearing techniques, but more information is becoming available on this subject all the time. Temperature, humidity, food, light and making things escape-proof are all subjects you will have to consider carefully with each new species that you try. Another popular thing to do is to set up a pond aquarium, much the same way as setting up a tropical fish tank, but without a heater. And remember, if your bugs don't look healthy, take them back to where you caught them, and let them go.

Of course, you should not forget about the potential of bug photography or even bug drawing. These activities require specialized equipment and a certain amount of practice, but there are plenty of good books on the market that can help you. With more and more sophisticated photo equipment available, professional quality bug photography is now possible with everyday equipment that you buy at an average camera store.

THE 125 COOLEST
BUGS
OF ALBERTA

EUROPEAN SKIPPER

Thymelicus lineola

Although the European Skipper is by far the most common summer butterfly in Edmonton, it is not a native of our area—it was accidentally introduced to eastern Canada from Europe and spread west from there. This butterfly possesses the distinctive skipper look, but it is more brightly orange and more inclined to hover than our other skippers. Amazingly, the presence of this introduced butterfly seems not to be affecting its local relatives. Because all of their caterpillars feed on grasses, there is plenty of food to go around. Skippers are fun to watch. They are fast flying and, quite frankly, cute. When a group of skippers assembles on a flower to sip nectar, they give the impression of being tiny, airborne teddy bears. When they chase each other in flight, they can be amazingly agile. To some people they look like moths, but all good bugsters should remember that a butterfly is nothing more or less than a sort of moth that flies by day. A skipper, in turn, is just a particular sort of butterfly with big eyes and a thick body. Admittedly, to appreciate skippers one has to be fond of subtle shades of orange and brown, but there is no law that says a butterfly has to be brightly coloured. There are 27 species of skippers in Alberta.

WINGSPAN: 25 mm.
RANGE: centred on Edmonton, but spreading outward.

CANADIAN TIGER SWALLOWTAIL

Papilio canadensis

Just as leaves appear on the poplar trees in May, out come Canadian Tiger Swallowtails from their pupae. Over the next few weeks, they mate and lay eggs, from which poplar-feeding caterpillars develop, complete with fake snake heads emblazoned on their smooth, green bodies. These big, bright butterflies are downright elegant in style, with soaring wingbeats and graceful lines. While they sip at flowers, they flutter their wings and dance on slender, black legs. This swallowtail is also one of the few butterflies with an attractive body, which is streamlined and luxuriantly furred in yellow and black. Even without its extravagant wings, it would be a noteworthy bug.

WINGSPAN: 100 mm.
RANGE: throughout Alberta.

As tropical butterfly houses become more popular, this butterfly gets noticed more often. Many times I have heard stories about visitors to these houses seeing their first swallowtail outside and rushing back in to report that one of the exotic beauties has escaped. And why do swallowtails have the "tails" on their hindwings? So that birds will grasp these conspicuous "appendages" and fly away with a beak full of membrane, rather than the butterfly itself. There are five species of swallowtails in Alberta.

27

CABBAGE WHITE

Pieris rapae

O ur least-loved butterfly is another European immigrant. Cabbage White caterpillars love nothing better than to drill through defence-less greens in a suburban vegetable garden, and when Europeans brought vegetables here from "the old country," they brought this butterfly, too. For many people, the Cabbage White is the most familiar butterfly of all, and it is certainly common in back alleys and places where other butterflies rarely venture. Up close, it is not a bad-looking creature, with subtle greens and yellows on a background of milky white. The white colour originally evolved as a warning to birds that this butterfly tastes bad, but because most of our Cabbage Whites grow up in gardens rather than among toxic wild weeds, they actually taste just fine. The similar Mustard White (*P. napi*) lives almost exclusively in natural areas and forests, where its caterpillars feed on wild members of the mustard family. Happily, it seems that the Cabbage White and the Mustard White stay out of each other's way—the country white and the city white, so to speak. There are about a dozen medium-sized, white butterflies in Alberta.

WINGSPAN: 50 mm.
RANGE: throughout Alberta.

CLOUDED SULPHUR

Colias philodice

S ulphurs are so named because most of them are yellow. For the same reason, they may also be responsible for the name "butter-fly." The Clouded Sulphur is by far the most common of the 12 species of sulphurs in Alberta, but where the other sulphurs also occur, identifying it can be a tricky chore indeed. Sulphurs are butterflies of open, sunny meadows and fields, and a great place to find Clouded Sulphurs is in an alfalfa field, where they sometimes fly in the thousands. They have a direct, powerful style of flight that really doesn't fit into the category of "fluttering." Males have solid black wing borders on the upper surface, while females have little yellow spots within the black. Clouded Sulphurs go through two or three generations during a typical Alberta butterfly season. The first to emerge are not the earliest butterflies of spring, but the last survivors are often the latest butterflies in fall. I have seen them up until the end of October when the weather stays warm, and there is a record of one at Bragg Creek on November 21!

WINGSPAN: 50 mm.
RANGE: throughout Alberta.

SPRING AZURE

Celastrina ladon

Bluebirds are fine for some people, but for those of us who love the smaller creatures, there is no more uplifting sight than the year's first Spring Azure. Flashing and dodging close to the ground, this lovely little butterfly is as iridescent as a tropical parrot and as bright as the April skies above. Later in the season, other species of "blues" will appear, with darker blue colours and more crisply marked underwings, but the Spring Azure is the one that comes out first, so it is the species we know and love the best. In fact, the Spring Azure is usually the first butterfly of the year to emerge from its pupa. Most of the other spring butterflies, such as Mourning Cloaks (p. 36) and Tortoise-shells, have spent the winter as adult butterflies tucked away under bark or among deadfall. By the time June rolls around, the last of the azures are looking grey and weatherbeaten. Most butterflies live only a week or two as adults, and their brief lives are usually squandered at the expense of their diminutive beauty. It is the males we see most often, because they fly whenever the sun is out, searching for females. There are 15 species of blue butterflies in Alberta.

WINGSPAN: 25 mm.
RANGE: throughout Alberta.

PURPLISH COPPER

Lycaena helloides

Anyone who takes an interest in butterflies will soon find that the subject is inexhaustable. Just when you think you have encountered all the butterfly types in your area, you notice a small, inconspicuous one, low to the ground. Most of the time it will be a copper, which is indeed a delight. Most of our 10 species of coppers are at least partly orange, and a combination of orange and brown markings gives them a semi-coppery look. Butterfly names being what they are, however, none of the coppers look as much like real copper as a copper-coloured beetle, but the name is still a good one. Our most common species is probably the Purplish Copper, the males of which have a purple iridescence. The Purplish Copper first appears in July, and in a warm year a second generation can also emerge in September. It is this second generation that can be really abundant, spreading into suburban neighbourhoods and sipping at the blossoms of that ever-popular butterfly flower, the good old dandelion. The almost identical Dorcas Copper (*L. dorcas*) lives in northern Alberta, as well as in the foothills and mountains.

WINGSPAN: 25 mm.
RANGE: southern Alberta.

MEADOW FRITILLARY

Boloria bellona

"Fritillary" is a confusing word. It refers to a large assortment of orange-and-black butterflies, and it can be pronounced either *FRIT-ill-erry* or *frit-ILL-err-ee*. To make things more complicated, there are also flowers called fritillaries, and in Europe all sorts of semi-related butterflies are called fritillaries. The Meadow Fritillary is one of the so-called "lesser" fritillaries, which are generally smaller than the "greater" fritillaries. Eleven species of lesser fritillaries emerge throughout Alberta's butterfly season. They are easy to find, because most of them have the enchanting habit of feeding while spreading their wings wide open to the sun. For this reason, they also make great subjects for nature photography. Some lesser fritillaries live in meadows in the forested regions, while others range far into the alpine zone at the tops of mountains. They don't seem to do well on the grassy prairies, but that is where the greater fritillaries come into their own. To tell a Meadow Fritillary from the other lesser "frits," look at the tips of its front wings. With a little imagination, they look like the point was snipped a bit short with a pair of scissors.

WINGSPAN: 40 mm.
RANGE: throughout Alberta, except in the southeastern prairies.

GREAT SPANGLED FRITILLARY

Speyeria cybele

This butterfly is the greatest of our greater fritillaries. On the upper side of the wings, greater fritillaries look much like lessers, but on the underside of the wings most of them have a dazzling array of bright silver spots. Because butterflies see things differently than people—much of what they see lies in the ultraviolet range   these spots are bright ultraviolet beacons to other fritillaries. At a distance, fritillaries attract one another with their appearance, but when they get close, they choose to communicate with perfumes instead. Sound familiar? Fritillary caterpillars, by the way, feed on the leaves of violets, and they only come out at night. In mid-summer, when the air is filled with fritillaries but the violets have finished blooming, it appears that there aren't enough violet leaves to go around. For those who like identification challenges, greater fritillaries fit the bill perfectly. We have nine species here, and some of them are so similar to one another that even experts can't seem to agree on what name to use. In fact, it is only the experts who fail to agree, because the rest of us don't even try.

> **WINGSPAN:** 60 mm.
> **RANGE:** south of the boreal forest and east of the mountains.

WHITE ADMIRAL

Liminitis arthemis

When you see the first White Admirals of the season, the school year is about to end. When I was young, I could hardly wait to get out of the classroom, grab my net, and go searching for the big beautiful admirals that were flapping past the windows during those last painful days of June. Even from my desk I could recognize them outside, because they are some of our most distinctive butterflies. A large black butterfly with a white band through the middle of both sets of wings pretty much has to be an admiral. Unless you live in the extreme southern part of the province, where the Weidemeyer's Admiral (*L. weidemeyerii*) and the Lorquin's Admiral (*L. lorquini*) are found, the White Admiral is the only expected species. The White Admiral is actually the western race of a species that is called the Red-spotted Purple in the East. The White Admiral also has red spots, but the Red-spotted Purple has no white, so perhaps this compromise is for the best. The name "admiral," by the way, was originally "admirable," which makes more sense. Too bad it faded from use.

WINGSPAN: 70 mm.
RANGE: throughout Alberta.

PEARL CRESCENT

Phyciodes tharos

Tiny, bright and proud—that's how I think of Pearl Crescents. These small butterflies fly with the grace and assurance of a majestic Monarch. Sometimes, they even glide, which is quite a feat at their size. They like to perch on sunlit leaves and spread their intricately patterned wings to the sky. It is in the southern parts of the province that you find the Pearl Crescent; in the northern two-thirds you find the almost identical Northern Crescent (*P. selenis*). These butterflies are so similar that the best way to distinguish between them is by their ranges. In fact, their other differences are so subtle that until recently they were thought to be the same species. Don't let their similarity discourage you from enjoying them, however. In mid-summer, crescents are among the commonest butterflies in Alberta, and they are easiest to find where they have shrubs on which to perch. As for telling the Pearl and the Northern from the other three small crescents in our province, well, that's a whole 'nother story best left to a different book.

WINGSPAN: about 30 mm.
RANGE: the southern half of Alberta.

MOURNING CLOAK

Nymphalis antiopa

I think the Mourning Cloak should be our provincial butterfly. There are two other species that have already been named after Alberta, but still, that's my opinion. After all, you can hope to see an unmistakable Mourning Cloak any time that the temperature rises above about 10° C, even in winter. The adults emerge in late July, at which point they are at their most magnificent: maroon with yellow trim and blazing blue highlights above and with a bark-coloured pattern on the underside. They are big butterflies, too. After feeding for a week or so, they go into a temporary dormancy, and then emerge to feed again in fall. When the snow comes, they tuck in under a chunk of bark, a shutter or a fallen log and hibernate. The first warm days of spring bring them back out of hiding, and that's when they mate and lay eggs. By the time June rolls around, there are still a few on the wing, although they are worn and tattered, with white wing fringes instead of yellow. An adult Mourning Cloak can live a full year, which is almost a year longer than most other butterflies.

WINGSPAN: 70 mm.
RANGE: throughout Alberta.

PAINTED LADY

Vanessa cardui

A lovely orange, black and white butterfly, swift on the wing and with a love for thistles—that's a Painted Lady. Often, I hear people say that butterflies used to be very common in the good old days, but now they have all but disappeared. Well, in some places that may be true, but usually these people are recalling a time when Painted Ladies arrived on migration, which is something that happens only once every 10 years or so. The populations of this butterfly build up in the southern U.S. over the course of a decade, until one year they swarm up into Canada by the bazillions. No thistle is safe from the egg-laying females, and an Alberta generation grows up over the summer. These Alberta-born butterflies, however, don't realize that they should return south in fall, so when winter arrives they all die, and we have to wait another 10 years to see them in such numbers again. There are a few Painted Ladies around every year, and sometimes the invasion goes on for two or three years at a time. Three similar "Ladies" occur in Alberta, but the Painted is by far the most common.

WINGSPAN: 55 mm.
RANGE: throughout Alberta.

37

RED ADMIRAL
Vanessa atalanta

Just as a dark butterfly with a white band through the wings is a White Admiral, a dark butterfly with a red band through the wings is a Red Admiral. The similarities end there, however, because these two butterflies are actually quite distantly related. The Red Admiral is a much closer cousin to the Painted Lady (p. 37), and, like her, it is a migratory butterfly that is only common every once in a while. Instead of thistles, Red Admiral caterpillars eat nettles, so you really have to admire the contribution they make to our summer environment. I like the way they choose a sunlit patch of ground and patrol it at high speed between basking periods on the ground or a tree trunk. Up close, you can see that this butterfly has a thick body, powerful flight muscles and stout, angular wings for rapid, super-controlled flight. When you find one in spring, it is usually quite worn and dull, with wing markings that are closer to pale orange than red. But when the summer generation emerges, their colours are dark and saturated, and the body is clothed in thick, brown hairs.

WINGSPAN: 50 mm.
RANGE: throughout Alberta.

COMMON WOOD NYMPH

Cercyonis pegala

You've undoubtedly already seen this butterfly, but you probably gave it little thought. Just about any grassy field will have at least a few Common Wood Nymphs fluttering around in July, bobbing at about the height of the tallest seed heads. Follow one, and you'll soon give up on getting a better look—it almost never sits still, and you rarely see this butterfly at a flower. On the wing, it is tough to tell this species from another four or five similar butterflies. Like all butterflies, however, it has to sleep eventually. The sun comes up mighty early in July, and the birds come up with it, searching for food among the dew-covered meadows. Wood nymphs, like other butterflies, don't start flying until much later in the morning—sometimes not until 10 a.m. or so—which means they spend five or more hours sitting in the open, hoping they don't get eaten. That's why they have a set of fake eyespots on their fore-

> **WINGSPAN:** about 60 mm.
> **RANGE:** the southern half of Alberta.

wings that can be flashed at a predator if the need arises. Birds are not too bright, and they often fall for the bluff, thinking they have disturbed the slumber of some glassy-eyed reptile. It really is too bad that these butterflies are not more inclined to show off their wings, because the males have a lovely purplish iridescence.

MONARCH

Danaus plexippus

The Monarch is our most famous butterfly, and one of our biggest as well. Most people know the story: Monarch are migrants, and our local population returns each winter to a small area west of Mexico City, where they spend the winter alongside the rest of the Monarchs from central and eastern North America. Not only that—the Monarchs that we see in Alberta are the grandchildren of the generation that overwintered in Mexico the year before. No one quite knows how these butterflies find their traditional wintering grounds, having never been there, but they do, and it impresses the heck out of everyone. They make the great migration against huge odds, but they are partly protected by their body chemistry. As a caterpillar, each Monarch feeds on the leaves of milkweed plants; chemicals in the leaves make both the caterpillar and the butterfly distasteful to birds. The distinctive orange and black colours on the Monarch advertise this protective ability, and another butterfly, the Viceroy (*Liminitis archippus*), copies the Monarch's colouring to help protect itself. Viceroys are smaller than Monarchs (only about 70 mm in wingspan)—in fact, they are the only species the Monarch is similar to—but the birds don't seem to notice their size.

WINGSPAN: about 95 mm.
RANGE: the southern two-thirds of Alberta.

POLYPHEMUS MOTH

Antheraea polyphemus

When a Polyphemus Moth comes flapping in to the porch light, everyone takes notice—many people assume it is a butterfly, because it is so amazingly beautiful. The antennae tell the real story: fuzzy or thin and pointy antennae all belong to moths; butterflies have slender antennae with thickened tips. The antennae of the male Polyphemus Moth are not feelers but smellers, and they pick up on the faint aroma of the female's perfume. Following the scent upwind, he finds his mate in the dark. When daylight comes, these moths generally roost with their wings above their backs. If a bird tries to peck at them, they suddenly spread the wings to expose the fake eyes on the wings. Most birds are startled by this display, but it doesn't fool all predators. Often, all you find of a Polyphemus is a pile of wings on the ground in the morning. The name "Polyphemus" comes from a one-eyed giant in Greek mythology—too bad the moth has four fake eyes and two real ones, for a total of six. Polyphemus caterpillars, by the way, are bright green, shaped like an extended accordion, and they feed on such things as birch and dogwood leaves. Because of its unique appearance, no other moth is easy to confuse with this one.

WINGSPAN: about 110 mm.
RANGE: throughout Alberta.

41

COLUMBIAN SILK MOTH

Hyalophora columbia

About the same size as a Polyphemus Moth (p. 41), this moth is less common. As such, it generates even more excitement when one appears around people. Along with the Polyphemus, it is a member of the giant silkworm family, a separate group from the commercial silkworm of Asia. At one point, the possibility of using giant silkworms for making silk for sale was explored in North America. It turned out that these silkworms wrap too many leaves and messy knots into their cocoons, so the plan failed, and the giant silkworms remain symbols of the wild. In more populated regions, they are gradually decreasing in numbers as habitat is destroyed and moths spend their lives flapping around light bulbs instead of mating and laying eggs. The rare Cecropia Moth (*H. cecropia*) in southeast Alberta is the only related species in our province. Adult giant silkworms are among the bugs that have no mouth and live off body reserves once they emerge from the pupa. If you find one, and it poops a light brown liquid, don't be alarmed. The liquid is "meconium" and consists of the wastes left over from the transformation from caterpillar to moth.

WINGSPAN: about 100 mm.
RANGE: throughout Alberta.

42

ONE-EYED SPHINX

Smerinthus cerysii

S phinx moths are named for the way their caterpillars adopt a pose something like the famous Sphinx of ancient Egypt. Another name for this group is "hawk moths," based on their streamlined form and rapid flight. I prefer "sphinx," because the moths, unlike hawks, are not predators. Most sphinx moths feed on flower nectar, but some, like the One-eyed Sphinx, are unable to feed as adults. They have no mouth. In this way, they are like the giant silkworm moths. The way they use the eye spots on their wings is also similar. The One-eyed is one of our most common species. Along

WINGSPAN: about 60 mm.
RANGE: throughout Alberta.

with its nearest relatives—there are four similar sphinx moths in Alberta— it rests during the day with the wings held at odd angles and turns up the tip of the abdomen (more so in the males). These things all work to break up the recognizable outline of the moth, so that birds will mistake it for a bit of bark or dry leaves. Among moths that fly at night, these sorts of camouflage methods are as diverse as the moths themselves.

BIG POPLAR SPHINX

Pachysphinx modesta

The first time I saw one of these impressive moths, I was a kid lying in bed at a cabin at Gull Lake. Suddenly something flew by the window, lit up by the yellow glow of the "bug-proof" light over the door. My first thought was "Hey, was that a tiny owl?" Then I realized, "Wait a minute! There's no such thing as a tiny owl!" A large female Big Poplar Sphinx probably has the heaviest body of any Alberta moth, and its caterpillar certainly qualifies as one of our biggest insects overall, weighing 14 g or more. The moth itself, however, is an unusual member of its family. Its wings are patterned in subtle pastel hues, camouflaged on the front wing and smeared with blue and red on the hindwings. Like the Twin-spotted Sphinx (*Smerinthus jamaicensis*), it does not feed as an adult. You might think that a big moth with caterpillars that eat poplar leaves would be common here. After all, the valleys of southern Alberta are filled with cottonwood trees, which are a type of poplar, and the northern forests are thick with aspen and balsam poplars. However, the Big Poplar Sphinx is still an uncommon find, and even experienced moth devotees are always thrilled when they see one.

WINGSPAN: about 110 mm.
RANGE: throughout Alberta.

SNOWBERRY CLEARWING

Hemaris diffinis

Another name for this little creature is the "Hummingbird Moth." Sure enough, when it hovers in front of a flower, uncoils its long, beak-like proboscis, and shows off its handsome colours, you can't blame some people for thinking they are looking at a bird. In bird field guides, this insect is usually the only one that warrants a picture. One friend of mine tells me that the first time she saw a Snowberry Clearwing, she crept up for a better look and then felt a deep sense of dread, because she realized she had no idea what sort of life-form she was looking at. Of course, no one should fear these moths, and in fact, they are quite delightful. They are members of the sphinx moth family, and unlike the others discussed in this book (pp. 43–46), they are fully able to feed. The only characteristics that set them apart from their relatives are the see-through wings and day-time habits; other sphinx moths are

> **WINGSPAN:** about 40 mm; the other species up to 60 mm.
> **RANGE:** throughout Alberta.

nocturnal. The caterpillars are typical of sphinxes, and they feed on a variety of forest plants. The adults are on the wing in May and June. There are two, possibly three species of very similar clear-winged sphinxes in Alberta, of which this one is the most common.

GALIUM SPHINX

Hyles gallii

T his moth is very streamlined and a powerful flier. With bright, attractive colours and big eyes, it seems to have more personality than most. The Galium Sphinx is one of those moths whose body is as handsome as its wings. Usually, you see these moths at night around lights, during the first half of the summer. Sometimes, however, they feed at flowers during the day, or at dusk, like a clear-winged sphinx (p. 45). Because they are so much bigger, they are even more likely to be mistaken for hummingbirds. The name "Galium" comes from one of the food plants for the caterpillars—also called "bedstraw" (early settlers supposedly stuffed their mattresses with it). The caterpillars will also feed on the leaves of fireweed. Some years, this species is quite abundant, while in others it is rare and hard to find. There are three similar species in Alberta. On the prairies, one of these species is the White-line Sphinx (*H. lineata*)—bigger with white veins on the forewing. As well, watch for the introduced Spurge Hawk Moth (*H. euphorbiae*). It looks a lot like a Galium, with lighter wing edges and more pink on the underwings. It was released here because it feeds on leafy spurge, which is a pest weed in many places.

WINGSPAN: about 65 mm.
RANGE: throughout Alberta.

GARDEN TIGER MOTH

Arctia caja

Tiger moths are not especially big, but this group includes some of the prettiest moths of all. The Garden Tiger Moth is one of the largest in Alberta. In a good year, it is easy to find in the southern part of the province. In the north, the St. Lawrence Tiger Moth (*Platarctia parthenos*) is more common—it has white splotches on the front wings rather than white, wavy lines. The bright colours of tiger moths are there to warn predators not to eat them—they are filled with bad-tasting chemicals. Of course, their warning colours only work during the day. At night, when the main enemies of tiger moths are bats, they defend them-selves in other ways. Some tiger moths can hear the bats coming, way above the range of human hearing.

WINGSPAN: about 55 mm.
RANGE: throughout Alberta.

When they feel threatened, they make their own ultrasonic sounds, to warn the bat that it is about to get a mouthful of bad-tasting tiger moth. Tiger moth caterpillars are generally fuzzy, and the fuzz can cause itchiness and rashes. The caterpillars even weave these hairs into their cocoons, so that the insect is protected at every stage of its life, both day and night.

47

SPOTTED TUSSOCK MOTH

Lophocampa maculata

This moth is one of those moths that is better known as a caterpillar— the familiar yellow-and-black "woolly bear." The caterpillars feed on willows, maples, birch and poplars, and they have white tufts of hairs set in the black bands on either end of the body. They are never important pests. Both the moth and the caterpillar are easy to recognize. The name "woolly bear," however, is more commonly used to refer to the caterpillar of the Isabella Moth (*Pyrrharctia isabella*), which is red and black, not yellow and black, and is not common in Alberta. Stories about how you can predict the length of the winter by the width of the woolly bear's red band are, of course, total "hooey." Unfortunately, so is the name "tussock moth," because real "tussock moths" belong in an entirely separate family, the Lymantriidae. The Spotted Tussock Moth is really a tiger moth. Thus, the woolly bear that isn't a woolly bear turns into a tussock moth that isn't a tussock moth. As tiger moths go, this moth is not a particularly colourful one, but it does have a nice yellowish-brown pattern with white splotches, and it is fairly common at lights in the first part of the summer.

WINGSPAN: about 45 mm.
RANGE: throughout Alberta.

POLICE CAR MOTH

Gnophaela vermiculata

This lovely moth is a member of the tiger moth family, in a subgroup that flies by day. They are easy to get close to, being clutzy fliers that beat their wings floppily in the mid-summer heat. Generally, poor fliers are also bad tasting, and that's why they can afford to make themselves easy targets for birds. The Police Car Moth really does look like an old-fashioned police car. It is black and white, with two little orange "lights" on the top of its thorax. This moth is tough to confuse with any other Alberta moth. The black wing veins make it easy to see how the wings are constructed, and like any moth or butterfly wing, they are amazingly strong. Between the veins, the wing membrane alternates from an upward angle to a downward angle, like corrugated roofing. This corrugation gives it strength. The body of a moth is also tougher than it looks, because the only way to teach birds not to eat Police Car Moths is to let them get a few mouthfuls of defence chemicals. If the moth can fly away after delivering its lesson to the bird, so much the better. The caterpillars of this moth are black, yellow and blue, and they feed on the leaves of lungwort.

> **WINGSPAN:** about 50 mm.
> **RANGE:** throughout Alberta but not on the prairies.

VIRGINIA CTENUCHA

Ctenucha virginica

When most people learn about this moth, their first obstacle is pronouncing the name. I say "ten-OOCH-ah," but I've heard things as outlandish as "coot-ENN-ee-YOU-tchah." These pronunciations are good examples of how *not* to coin an English name—simply turning the scientific name inside out doesn't always work. In most ways, this moth is reminiscent of the Police Car Moth (p. 49), and it, too, is a member of the tiger moth family. Ctenuchas emerge earlier in the summer than Police Car Moths, and if you catch a female and put her in a paper bag, you'll be amazed at how many eggs she can lay. The caterpillars feed on grasses and sedges, while the adults flutter at flowers and sip nectar. They fly by day and are easy to find in open areas and meadows. There are no other moths in Alberta closely related to this one. The black-and-blue coloration of this moth is—you guessed it—another sort of warning to birds that these moths taste terrible. Iridescent blue is an uncommon warning colour this far north, but in the Central and South American tropics it is as common a warning colour as yellow, red and black are here. Thus, we have an exotic moth with an exotic name, perfectly at home in Alberta.

WINGSPAN: about 50 mm.
RANGE: throughout Alberta, except on the prairies.

FOREST TENT CATERPILLAR MOTH

Malacosoma disstria

E very seven to eleven years, you just can't miss this moth. The caterpillars are nice enough to look at one at a time, with pretty blue markings and little tufts of hairs. When they appear by the billions, however, their appeal wears thin. They can strip entire aspen forests of their leaves, leaving them wintry and bleak, festooned only with the cocoons of their destructors, which are about the size and shape of small, furry perogies. When the moth comes out, most people do not associate it with the famous caterpillar, but it is an easily recognizable creature, with warm brown fur and smallish wings. Of course, the forests do recover from these outbreaks of caterpillars, and the outbreaks have been going on for millions of years. As the caterpillars become more and more common, so do their predators and parasites, which eventually brings things into balance. At the height of an outbreak,

WINGSPAN: about 35 mm.
RANGE: throughout Alberta.

some sorts of birds have so much to eat that they do especially well in the breeding season. We suspect that some rare species, such as the Black-billed Cuckoo, actually expand their range when the caterpillars are at a high point, and then fade away between caterpillar outbreaks. There are two species of tent caterpillars in Alberta.

51

BLACK WITCH

Ascalapha odorata

The Black Witch is our largest moth, but it's not really "ours," in a way. Every summer, a few of these impressive creatures turn up in Alberta, flying to lights. Would you believe that each one of these moths was born somewhere in Central America? The Black Witch is a tropical species that disperses widely in all directions each and every year. On powerful elongated wings, it makes its way north, becoming less and less common the further into Canada one goes. It shouldn't surprise anyone to notice that the ones we find here in Alberta are generally worn and faded, with torn wing edges and dull colours. To fuel their incredibly long journey—longer, by the way, than the flight of an Alberta Monarch butterfly (p. 40) to its wintering grounds in Mexico—the moths feed each night, on sap or rotting fruit. Thus, they are drawn to the same sort of baits that attracts underwings (pp. 53–54), and in fact they are the largest members of the underwing subfamily of the owlet moths. Don't let their lack of a colourful hindwing fool you— they are still closely related. Males have longer, more pointed wings, while females have a light band through the middle of the wings.

WINGSPAN: up to 150 mm.
RANGE: wherever its wings can carry it.

WHITE UNDERWING

Catocala relicta

The underwings are moths of late summer. On occasion you see them by day, but for the most part they are creatures of early evening, when they search for sap-flows and over-ripe fruit, on which they feed. Their coloration is remarkable, with camouflaged front wings and boldly coloured rear wings. There are 12 species of underwings in Alberta, but only this one is black and white. At rest, closing its front wings over the hind ones, the White Underwing blends in perfectly with the bark of the paper birch tree. If a bird discovers it, the moth spreads its wings and takes advantage of the bird's brief surprise to escape. If you want to see one of these moths, here's

WINGSPAN: about 65 mm.
RANGE: throughout Alberta.

what to do: mix up a pot of beer, molasses, rum and lots of brown sugar. Warm this mixture up to melt the sugar, then let it cool. Go outside and paint the mixture on the rough bark of poplar trees, and then wait until after dark. Sneak up carefully with a flashlight, and try not to snap any twigs. The moths have good hearing, and they will sometimes flee at the slightest sound. Of course, after an hour or so of sipping the alcoholic bait, they seem less concerned about people, and more absorbed in their own inebriated thoughts.

ONCE-MARRIED UNDERWING

Catocala unijuga

This species is more of a typical underwing, with the hindwings patterned in red and black. The pattern makes them easy to recognize as a group, but in Alberta there are eight species that are so similar even the moth experts can't always agree on which is which. In some ways, this confusion only adds to the mystique that surrounds this group. In total, there are 12 species of underwings in Alberta. A set of strange names for the Alberta underwings conjures images of bitter male entomologists who had difficulty with the women in their lives: the Once-married Underwing is joined in Alberta by such species as the Mother Underwing, the Charming Underwing and the Forsaken Underwing. Elsewhere, you can find the Widow Underwing, the Girlfriend Underwing, the Sorrowful Underwing, the Betrothed Underwing, the Old Maid Underwing, the Consort Underwing, the Bride Underwing and the Old Wife Underwing. I guess the lesson here, to avoid the pain of love lost, is to spend more time with one's partner and less time out prowling in the dark. Unless, of course, you both like underwings, in which case you can enjoy looking for them together. Underwing caterpillars, by the way, are streamlined and camouflaged, and most of them feed on poplars.

WINGSPAN: about 70 mm.
RANGE: throughout Alberta.

PALE BEAUTY

Campaea perlata

H ow pale, and how beautiful! The broad, butterfly-like wings of this familiar moth are a lovely translucent green. Its slender body struggles to flap the wings, and thus it doesn't whir in flight like most moths, it flutters. In fact, there are only three obvious signs that this one is not a butterfly. First, it has thin antennae, with no clubs at the tips. Second, it flies by night. Third, it has a habit of crashing into leaves and branches when it flies, rather than deftly avoiding them. The Pale Beauty is a member of a large group of equally enchanting moths, the geometers. They are also called "inchworm moths," because it is their caterpillars that do the familiar inching along when they travel, which is a result of having legs at the front and

> **WINGSPAN:** about 40 mm.
> **RANGE:** throughout Alberta.

back of the body but not in the middle. Some people call them "loopers," for the same reason. Many of the geometers are colourful, and some even fly by day. Almost always, when someone comes to me with a "butterfly that isn't in the field guides," it turns out to be a geometer. There are at least 250 species of geometers in Alberta, but only a few are pale green, and this one is the biggest of the greenies.

CLAYBANK TIGER BEETLE

Cicindela limbalis

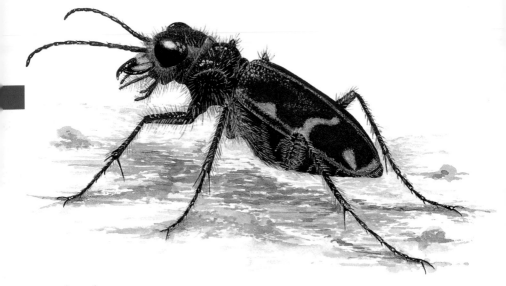

Tiger beetles are exciting. They have long legs and large eyes, and they run fast and have powerful jaws for killing other bugs. Some, as an added bonus, are brightly coloured. The Claybank Tiger Beetle is one of our finest, with deep iridescent reds and shining green trim. These beetles live on bare clay slopes, such as the slumping banks along many rivers. They generally like open ground with few plants, because they find it easy in such places to spot prey and run it down. There are 19 species of tiger beetles in Alberta, but most people don't get a chance to see them, which is a shame. Why? The reason is simple—the beetles always see us first. They are quick to take wing, but they usually don't fly far. It's easy to watch where they land, and sneak up for a good look. If you watch a tiger beetle, you'll see it chase down food, zip out after potential mates, and attack any small piece of debris that might be an edible bug. They only come out on sunny days, mind you, so don't go looking for them in the rain—that's the time to look for water beetles.

LENGTH: 12 mm.
RANGE: throughout Alberta.

56

PURPLE-RIMMED CARABUS

Carabus nemoralis

Have you ever sat in your garden on a warm spring evening, and wondered what sorts of creatures are rustling around in the dry leaves? Whatever I imagine, it turns out to be the Purple-rimmed Carabus every time—big black beetles with a lovely bit of iridescent purple around the edges of their bodies. They come out mainly at night, and they eat other insects, slugs and worms. Thus, they are generally a good thing to have in your yard. There are about 10 species of similar-sized ground beetles in Alberta. When early shipments of ore, from North America to Europe, reached their destination, the sailors would fill the hold with dirt from European shores. In it, there were beetles such as the carabus, and many of these stowaways have become common in Canada and the United States. The Purple-rimmed Carabus is remarkably well-suited to life in the city, and it is not found in natural areas. Apparently, our suburban gardens remind it of home. Pick one up and it will release a scent something like rotten fruit. Be careful of its jaws! These beetles don't bite unless provoked, but they have the jaws of a predator, and they'll pinch you if you pinch them.

LENGTH: 22 mm.
RANGE: within the major cities.

57

FIERY HUNTER

Calosoma calidum

This beetle is a lot like the Purple-rimmed Carabus (p. 57), but in many ways it is even more impressive. For one thing, it is a lot more curvaceous. For another, it has dozens of ruby-red jewel spots set in its shining black wing covers. They really do look like jewels, even under a magnifying glass. And while the Purple-rimmed Carabus likcs to rummage around among the dead leaves, the Fiery Hunter is also a fearless climber of trees. Day and night, it explores the poplar woods for its favourite food—caterpillars. Even fuzzy tent caterpillars are to its liking. With mighty jaws and a head as hard as a choke cherry pit, the Fiery Hunter chews through the caterpillar's hairy defences, and gobbles up the soft insides. This beetle is a native species, and one we can be proud of. Watch for the similar Frostbitten Hunter (*C. frigidum*), which looks a lot like the Fiery Hunter but is slimmer where the wing covers join the pronotum. As well, notice that you will sometimes find these beetles with green or golden, rather than red, jewel spots. These ones are not a different species, just a different variation on a lovely little theme. However, there are about 10 species of similar-sized ground beetles in Alberta.

LENGTH: 20 mm.
RANGE: throughout Alberta.

SIDEWALK CARABID

Pterostichus melanarius

"C arabid" is the name given to any member of the noble family of ground beetles. In Alberta alone, there are as many species of ground beetles as there are birds. The Sidewalk Carabid is one of our most well known, because it does, indeed, appear quite regularly on the sidewalk in typical suburban neighbourhoods. This beetle is another introduced species, like the Purple-rimmed Carabus (p. 57), that came to North America in ship ballasts. The first American records are from 1926. Unlike many other alien invaders, the Sidewalk Carabid is slowly spreading into the countryside surrounding the major cities, where it manages to eke out a living along-

LENGTH: 15 mm.
RANGE: mostly in and around major cities.

side its native relatives. This ground beetle is by no means our biggest or most spectacular, but it's one that everyone should know. When you think that the average size of a beetle is about 2.5 mm, the Sidewalk Carabid takes its rightful place as one of the biggies at 15 mm. Like most of its relatives, it is a predator. It is a friend of the gardener and terror of insect life in the flowerbeds.

STAG-JAWED CARABID

Passimachus elongatus

Yes, I know—stags don't have big jaws, they have big antlers. Stag beetles, on the other hand, have big jaws that happen to look like antlers. We don't have any big-jawed stag beetles in Alberta, but we do have a ground beetle that many people mistake for one. The easy way to tell the two apart is to look at the antennae—stag beetles have elbowed, many-leaved antennae while those of carabids are straight and thin. Don't be concerned about confusing Stag-jawed Carabids with other ground beetles—among the Alberta ground beetles, this one is hard to misidentify. To find this mean-looking, purple-trimmed marvel, go to a patch of bald-butt prairie where

LENGTH: 25 mm.
RANGE: restricted to sandy prairies in the southeast.

the soil is sandy. Then start looking under old fence posts or dried cow pies. When you find the beetle, be careful how you pick it up. It can bite hard, because it uses its jaws for killing other bugs, not just for fighting over girls. You might also look for these beetles at night with a flashlight, but make sure to ask permission from the rancher before you start prowling around his or her pasture in the dark. Burrowing Owls also like to use this sort of habitat, and one sometimes finds many pieces of half-digested Stag-jawed Carabid in their regurgitated pellets.

BURYING BEETLE

Nicrophorus sp.

S omebody has to deal with them, and you know exactly what I am talking about. Yes, I'm referring to dead mice. Without nature's help, the world would be knee deep in them. That is where the beautiful, orange-and-black Burying Beetles fit into the grand scheme of things. Flying low over the ground, just before sundown, they spread their many-leaved antennae to the wind and sniff. They seek the unmistakable aroma of today's death. If they find a big carcass, such as a deer or a coyote, they join their carrion-eating buddies for a quick snack. On the other hand, if they find a dead mouse, or some other tiny corpse, they rejoice. A female Burying Beetle's dream is to find a dead mouse, and a husband, all in the same evening. Then, it can

LENGTH: 12–20 mm.
RANGE: throughout Alberta.

bury the treasure, kill the maggots that might steal some of the meal, and push the cadaver into a ball. Next, it lays its own eggs, and starts a family. The beetle grubs raise their little heads to beg for food, and in response Mom and Dad give them bits of putrescence to eat. Now isn't that nice? Who said that beetles don't possess the ability to show complex behaviour and tender parental care? There are 10 species of these caring Burying Beetles in Alberta.

HAIRY ROVE BEETLE

Creophilus maxillosus

To most people, a rove beetle doesn't look much like a beetle at all. It is a long, slender insect, and its wing covers are short. But a beetle it is, and a good one at that. Beneath those wing covers are full-sized wings, folded so intricately that you'd swear they couldn't fit. The Hairy Rove Beetle is another one of those bugs that is attracted to death. Any carcass will do, and they are some of the first creatures to arrive after decomposition has set in. The Hairy Rove Beetle is not there to eat the meat, mind you. Instead, it is there to ambush the unwary. After all, a dead animal is a magnet for bugs. So the large Hairy Rove Beetle prowls the cadaver and dines on flies, maggots and various other beetles. Rove beetles form a diverse family of beetles, but most are very small. Only five or six really large rove beetles exist in the province. One of these whoppers, known as the Pie-Killer (*Ontholestes cingulatus*), prefers to do its fly hunting on top of cow and bison "pies." When it feels threatened, it curls its long abdomen up over its back, and exposes yellow bands between the segments, making it look frighteningly like a yellow jacket wasp.

LENGTH: up to 20 mm.
RANGE: throughout Alberta.

MAY BEETLE

Phyllophaga spp.

The first thing to know about May Beetles is that you don't always see them in May. May is, however, the best month to find them, and they are tough to ignore when you do. These beetles are big, fat, clumsy, stupid ones that fly around at night, and they are strongly attracted to lights. So, when you are sitting outside on that first warm evening in the spring, you hear something like, *Bzzzzh... bzzzahsssszzzzzzzzzzzzzzzss... PFUT! bzt. bzt! Bzzzzzt!... bzzhssssss... bzt.* That's the sound of a May Beetle on a collision course with the porch light, after which it falls on its back and can't find its feet. Kids like them, because you can find them in the morning, and they are fun to play with—they don't eat once they become beetles, which means they don't bite. You might have some competition finding these beetles from hungry birds. May Beetle grubs grow up underground, where they feed on roots for three whole years. However, they are never common enough here to be real pests. These are members of the grand and glorious scarab beetle family, and they share with other scarabs such features as spiny legs, a sturdy body and many-leaved antennae. There are four very-similar species of May Beetles in Alberta, plus six smaller look-alikes.

LENGTH: 15–20 mm.
RANGE: throughout Alberta.

TEN-LINED JUNE BEETLE

Polyphylla decemlineata

T his beetle is our largest scarab. The antennae are especially awesome on this beetle, especially on the males. They look a bit like moose antlers, but being many-leaved, they give the impression of a bull moose with seven sets of antlers all stacked up on one another. When the beetle spreads this magnificent fan to the wind, the scent it seeks is that of the female. These beetles do not live long once they emerge, and they spend all of their time searching for mates and laying eggs. In general, the life history of this species is much like that of the May Beetles (p. 63), although the Ten-lined June Beetle quite naturally comes out mainly in July. The colour pattern of this beetle is also fascinating. If you look closely, with a magnifying glass, you'll see that the stripes on the wing covers are made up of tiny overlapping scales.

LENGTH: 25 mm.
RANGE: in the southern prairies, in places with sandy soil.

The scales are pointed at one end, and rounded at the other, and some are white, while others are tan. They are set in a background of amber-coloured cuticle, and each scale is as polished as a piece of hard wax. On the underside of the body, scales mix with long, beige hairs to give the beetle an almost cuddly look. There are two species of lined June beetles in Alberta—the second is about half the size of the Ten-lined.

GOLD DUST BUPRESTID

Buprestis confluenta

Among those who love beetles, another famous family is the metallic wood-borers. Scientists call them "buprestids," and because this word is so delightful, I use it, too. Many of these insects are large, iridescent and almost robotic in their movements. They thrive in the heat of summer, and the best place to find them is on the sunlit sides of trees, where they meet their mates and lay the eggs that will become their "flathead borer" larvae. One of the finest metallic wood-borers in Alberta is the Gold Dust Buprestid. Because its larvae live inside dead or dying poplar trees, it is widespread. The adult beetle is a lovely iridescent spring green, with yellow speckles all over the wing covers. Once you learn where to look for them, you'll find buprestids in most places that have trees (and even some that don't). There are about 60 species of buprestids in Alberta. In the southwest corner of the province, watch for the Golden Buprestid (*B. aurulenta*), with its orange-trimmed, scintillating green body. In the jack pine forests of the north, the superlative species is the Sculptured Pine Borer (*Chalcophora virginiensis*), a really big one that looks like it was made from hammered brass.

LENGTH: 17 mm.
RANGE: the southern half of Alberta.

RESPLENDANT CLICK BEETLE

Ctenicera resplendens

Among all of our iridescent beetles, it would be tough to pick the brightest. Still, some Resplendant Click Beetles are serious contenders for this title. These beetles are certainly the most colourful click beetles in Alberta, varying from bright green to almost copper-coloured. The Resplendant Click is one of the few click beetles in Alberta that is identifiable at a glance. The click beetle family is one big group of beetles—there are roughly 130 species of click beetles in Alberta—and most of them are confusingly similar, in a generally brown and featureless way. Still, they all share the amazing characteristic that gives the family its name—the "click." Turn one over on its back, and it will flail with its legs for a moment or two.

LENGTH: 13 mm.
RANGE: throughout Alberta.

Then, it arches its body, and suddenly *PUNG*, it flips end over end into the air and, like a tossed coin, lands back on its feet roughly half of the time. The truth is, however, this flipping motion is probably not why these beetles click. In nature, it is doubtful that they fall on their backs on a perfectly flat surface very often. Instead, the click probably functions to startle predators. Some types of click beetles can use the click to launch themselves into the air even when they are upright.

SAPPHIRE-WINGED CLICK BEETLE

Ctenicera aeripennis

In the forested areas of Alberta, these beetles are big, beautiful and harmless. The iridescent blue wing covers and jet black head and pronotum are unmistakable. In the prairies, however, the beetles are smaller and dull-coloured, and their larvae are pests, called "Prairie Grain Wireworms." The larvae dig around in the soil and eat the roots of cereal crops. I don't want to appear unsympathetic to farmers, but the truth is that any adult click beetle is a wonder of nature, no matter how despicable its children might be. Most click beetle larvae, by the way, are not pests. To find click beetles, look on the leaves of plants during the months of May and June. They are

LENGTH: 17 mm in the forests; 13 mm on the prairies.
RANGE: throughout Alberta.

active during the day, and they are usually easy to spot as you move slowly— the way expert bug watchers always do. The sure field mark of a click beetle is the way the hind corners of the pronotum are extended into little backward pointing spines, framing the shoulders of the wing covers. Once you recognize their body form, you'll find it easy to identify this family of beetles. There are 130 species of click beetles in Alberta, but the Sapphire-winged Click Beetle is easy to recognize.

BEER BEETLE

Glischrochilus quadrisignatus

I realize that not everyone reading this book will be a beer drinker, but for those of you who are, you'll know this beetle for sure. Imagine yourself on the patio, tossing back a frosty mug of draft. Suddenly, swimming in the suds, you discover a handsome black beetle with a few orange spots. It's a Beer Beetle! You fish it out with your finger, flick it away, and realize that another one has taken the plunge. These beetles get in people's hair and run around on the table, and if you know something about them, they can be a great source of conversation. They certainly do no harm. Beer Beetles (some people call them sap beetles, but I'm not sure what *they've* been drinking) are naturally attracted to things like rotting fruit that lies fermenting on the ground. It might come as a surprise to some people to discover that we humans did not invent alcohol. In fact, rotting fruit can become about as potent as light beer, but generally these beetles don't drown in rotting fruit. There are five species of Beer Beetles in Alberta.

LENGTH: about 6 mm.
RANGE: throughout Alberta.

STINK BEETLE

Eleodes hispilabris

During mid-summer on the prairies, in the southeast corner of Alberta, things can get a mite hot. So what in tarnation is a big black beetle doing, running around on the sun-baked ground during the heat of the day? These insects seem to thrive in deserts, and their black colour somehow doesn't make them heat up as much as we might think they would. They are members of the darkling beetle family, a group that includes the familiar Meal Worm Beetle (*Tenebrio molitor*) that is often sold for pet food and fish bait. There are seven similar-sized darkling beetles in Alberta. Stink Beetles get their name by doing head stands and puffing smelly gas out their back ends, if you disturb them. Some cheat, mind you, and do the headstand without the puff. This feature has not been studied yet in Alberta, so if you don't mind smelling some beetle butts, perhaps this is the entomological project for you. One thing is clear, however—they don't have much to fear from most predators, or they wouldn't be walking around in the open all day.

LENGTH: 20 mm.
RANGE: restricted to the southeastern prairies.

NUTTALL'S BLISTER BEETLE

Lytta nuttalli

H ere we have yet another good-looking iridescent beetle, coloured in lovely greens, reds and blues. If you are a bird, this pattern makes sense—they all taste terrible. However, in the case of the blister beetle family (most of which are dull grey or black), the terrible-tasting chemical is something called "cantharidin." This poison is quite potent, causing blistering wherever it encounters moist skin, such as the inside of your mouth or an open sore. Toads can eat them without any difficulty, but most other animals would rather eat hornets or hot coals. If you have ever heard of Spanish Fly (a so-called aphrodisiac), you might find it interesting that the "fly" is actually a closely related blister beetle from Europe (*L. vesicatoria*). Nuttall's Blister Beetles feed on pea-family plants, and they are easy to find in early summer. The males are much smaller than the females, and they mate end-to-end. There must be some sort of attachment hooks in there somewhere, because it is common to find females dragging dead males behind them, still in the act of copulation. Presumably, the female can dislodge her deceased partner—it would be difficult to lay her eggs with his body in the road. There are 26 species of blister beetles in Alberta, but only three large, iridescent ones.

LENGTH: females up to 22 mm.
RANGE: throughout Alberta.

SEVEN-SPOT LADYBUG

Coccinella septempunctata

Ladybugs eat aphids, and because aphids eat crops and garden plants, many people consider ladybugs good. Back in the 1950s, entomologists figured that more kinds of ladybugs would mean more goodness, so they brought the Seven-spot over from Europe and released hundreds of them on the east coast of the United States. The Seven-spots spread happily across the continent, gobbling aphids, and now this ladybug is one of the most common species in Canada and the United States. Not surprisingly, however, there are still lots of aphids here. The only obvious effect of the Seven-spot's arrival has been the decline of some native species of ladybugs. Perhaps the Seven-spot out-competes them, or eats their eggs, or spreads disease—no one knows for sure. To those of us who care about our native ladybugs, the Seven-spot is now the bad guy. It's hard to be too angry with them, mind you. After all, they are still ladybugs, and among beetles the ladybugs are almost everyone's favourites. It's just too bad that we think of them as little employees, sent out into the fields to do a job for us by killing our pests. Like us, they are just trying to make a living. There are about 35 species of ladybugs in Alberta.

LENGTH: 7 mm.
RANGE: throughout Alberta.

71

TWO-SPOT LADYBUG

Adalia bipunctata

"There are ladybugs in my house, and it's the middle of winter—what should I do?" Entomologists hear this question quite often, and most of the time the ladybugs turn out to be Two-spots. They get into your house in the fall, looking for a comfy place to hibernate. Then, somewhere in January or February, some of them figure it must be spring, so they start looking for a way out. If you find these misguided beetles on your window panes, you can put them in a cooler place in the house and hope they go back to sleep, or you can offer them a small morsel of liver-flavoured cat food as a snack. Apparently, to them it tastes like aphids. Of course, if you have any aphids on your house plants, the ladybugs prefer them to the cat food.

LENGTH: 4 mm.
RANGE: throughout Alberta.

The Two-Spot is a lovely native species, and it is also amazingly variable. Most have two black spots on a red background, while others have four spots or two red shoulder patches on a black background. After a while, you can recognize them across the length of a room, just by their size and shape, despite the fact that there are about 35 other species of ladybugs in Alberta.

THIRTEEN-SPOT LADYBUG

Hippodamia tredecimpunctata

Like all beetles, ladybugs begin life as an egg and then hatch into a larva. The larva of a ladybug looks something like a long-legged caterpillar, and it eats the same thing as the adult—aphids. Between the larval stage and the adult stage, there is a resting pupal stage, as with all beetles. The Thirteen-spot Ladybug is a native species, and it is common in grassy fields, lawns and gardens. Unlike many of its relatives, it is orange rather than red, and it is more elongate than most other ladybugs as well. There are about 35 species of ladybugs in Alberta, so look for certain features when identifying them: the colour, the arrangement and number of spots, the pattern on the pronotum and the overall shape of the beetle. The thing that confuses some people is that a Thirteen-spot Ladybug is not just an older, bigger Two-spot Ladybug, but that it is a separate sort of critter altogether, a separate species. Once ladybugs emerge from the pupa, they don't change their spots, nor do they grow in size. They also don't change their spots when the weather changes, as some people once believed. What a strange view of nature! As if one creature exists only to help another one survive—the ultimate in selflessness. Sorry, it just isn't true.

LENGTH: 6 mm.
RANGE: throughout Alberta.

73

SPRUCE SAWYER

Monochamus scutellatus

Everyone who loves beetles dreams of the tropics. There, most of the beetles are much like our own, except that the biggest ones are much, much bigger. It is a thrill, then, to find a beetle in your own backyard that is a miniature replica of the great *Batocera* longhorn beetles of Asia and Australia. The Spruce Sawyer—there are two species of these beetles in Alberta—has an exotic look, with its white-flecked ebony body, elegant shape and long, curved antennae. The male's antennae are longer than the female's, but the female is a bigger beetle overall. These marvelous creatures emerge in mid-summer, from pupae that are formed just below the bark, inside dead spruce trees. The larvae excavate long, winding galleries through the wood, and somehow the long-"horned" adults chew their way out of the wood without harming their antennae or their slender legs. When they take flight to find a mate, they are noisy and awkward, flying with their legs splayed out to the sides, and their bodies held straight up and down. When one accidentally crashes into a car or a person, the northern forests predictably ring with the cry, "What the HECK is THAT?"

LENGTH: 20 mm, not counting the antennae.
RANGE: within the forested areas of Alberta, where there are spruce trees.

DOGBANE BEETLE

Chrysochus auratus

This beetle is another one of those insects that is so darn pretty you really can't walk past it without a second glance. It looks like a great big, carefully polished, bright green ladybug. Its body is round and plump, and its legs end in what might well be described as paws. In other words, it's a cute beetle and a gorgeous one as well. The Dogbane Beetle is a member of the leaf beetle family, and there are about 215 species of leaf beetles in Alberta. However, the Dogbane is the only one

LENGTH: 10 mm.
RANGE: throughout Alberta but more common in the southern half.

so big and bright green. And, surprise, surprise, it eats leaves, particularly the leaves of dogbane and milkweed. These plants produce toxic chemicals to discourage animals from eating them. This beetle also has chemical defences, and it will ooze droplets of distasteful liquid when grasped. The Dogbane Beetle's first line of defence, however, is the same as most other leaf beetles— it tucks its legs in and drops to the ground. This beetle is one of those insects whose numbers fluctuate greatly from year to year. I saw some from time to time in the early 1970s, when I was a bug-crazed youth but then not again until the 1990s. So my advice to you is, enjoy them when you see them!

GOLDEN TORTOISE BEETLE

Deloyala guttata

To find this outstanding beetle, look on the leaves of wild morning glory plants in mid-summer. You can't miss the tortoise beetles—they really do look like they have been adorned with little bits of gold leaf. To me, the combination of a golden beetle, the lovely white flowers of the morning glory and the sunny hillsides where they grow is a classic nature scene for Alberta. To beetle watchers and photographers, this one is hard to beat. To collectors, however, it is a huge disappointment, because the gold fades away as soon as the beetle is dead. Tortoise beetles form a subgroup within the leaf beetle family. There are four species of tortoise beetles in Alberta, and they are easy to recognize by their body shape, which is like a little upside-down bowl. Through the semi-transparent edges of this living shield, you can see their legs and head. The feet are well-adapted for sticking firmly to the spearhead-shaped leaves of the morning glory. If an ant finds the tortoise beetle and tries to attack, the beetle simply grabs onto the leaf, pulls its shield down around its body, and gives the ant nothing at all to grab onto.

LENGTH: 5 mm.
RANGE: the southern half of Alberta.

STRAWBERRY ROOT WEEVIL

Otiorhynchus ovatus

The Strawberry Root Weevil is one of our most familiar beetles, but no one would ever say it was spectacular. In fact, it is remarkable mainly for its dullness. The weevil family is the largest family of beetles in the world, and its members are known for their long "noses" that are actually more like muzzles, with jaws on the end. The Strawberry Root Weevil is part of the subgroup called "the blunt-nosed weevils." Overall, there are about 205 species of Alberta weevils, about 25 of which are "blunt-nosed." All Strawberry Root Weevils are females, and they give birth exclusively to more females. As well, they do not fly. In fact, their wing covers are fused together. Instead, they walk, and they walk to the darndest places. You find them inside houses, up in lamps, in your car—you name it. As a kid, I remember falling asleep while watching them crawl slowly across the walls. Next time you see one, look around for a strawberry root, the food of this beetle's larva. I'll bet you don't see one. I once calculated how far a Strawberry Root Weevil could go if it walked 12 hours a day for its entire adult life, and I came up with something like 10 km.

LENGTH: 5 mm.
RANGE: throughout Alberta.

WOOD ANT

Formica spp.

Ants are social creatures, and for this reason it is impossible to prevent some people from comparing them to us. In my opinion, this comparison is a mistake. For one thing, ant societies are made up almost entirely of females that never reproduce. Imagine that in human terms, and hopefully you'll stop the comparison right there. If you need further convincing, picture a society where there is only one mother, and she gives birth dozens of times every day. There are at least 21 species of wood ants in Alberta, but I grew up believing that there are two kinds of ants—red and black—and they are constantly at "war" with one another. Well, that's baloney, too! Have a look at the average Wood Ant. First, it is both red *and* black. Second, if you look closely at one of the ant hills that these insects live in, you will sometimes see black ants running around among the red-and-black ones.

LENGTH: 4–8 mm.
RANGE: throughout Alberta.

These ants are slaves, or more accurately, they were stolen from their own colony when they were still pupae, and when they hatched they figured they were among others of their own kind. So they do work for their captors, and everyone is happy. Now is that different from humanity, or am I just a mixed-up entomologist?

CARPENTER ANT

Camponotus spp.

It's nice to live in Alberta because we have no termites. Termites are interesting, mind you, but some kinds do have the habit of devouring houses. When Albertans talk about termites they really mean Carpenter Ants, which are the biggest ants in the province. Luckily, they are also slow moving and not particularly aggressive. They have no sting, and like Wood Ants (p. 78), their main defence is to bite. Their jaws are strong, because they chew through wood for a living, which is how they are similar to termites. In the wild, you can spot a Carpenter Ant nest in a tree trunk by the pile of sawdust outside the entrance. These ants sometimes build their homes inside the woodwork of older houses, and here again the thing to watch for is sawdust. They don't actually eat the wood, but in the course of excavating their galleries, they certainly do weaken it, to the point where the tree, or the

LENGTH: about 12 mm.
RANGE: the forested areas of Alberta.

expensive house, may "fail," as the engineers say. Woodpeckers love to eat these ants, and it is fitting that our biggest ant is continually under attack from our biggest woodpecker, the Pileated Woodpecker. There are three species of Carpenter Ants in Alberta.

79

NEVADA BUMBLEBEE

Bombus nevadensis

Bumblebees have a painful sting, but they are so cute and fuzzy that we love them just the same. They are slow to anger and quite docile, even when you are near their nests. In spring, queens set up new colonies in the abandoned burrows of mice and voles. There, they make wax pots, with open tops. Inside these pots, they rear their grubs. Once the grubs grow up to be worker bees, the number of pots increases, and some are used to rear the young while others are filled with pollen or honey. Bumblebees visit flowers to gather both pollen and nectar. Their wings are so small for the size of their bodies that some biologists were unsure for a while about how they could possibly fly. Bumblebee bodies look bigger than they are—all that hair is deceptive. The hair helps hold body heat when the bumblebees fly, and they can fly at lower temperatures than many other bees. One friend of mine claims that when the bumblebees come out in the spring, so do the bears, and when the bees go in for the winter, the bears do, too. The Nevada Bumblebee is one of about 35 species in Alberta.

LENGTH: 20 mm.
RANGE: throughout Alberta.

BLUE HORNTAIL

Sirex cyaneus

Horntails are our largest sawflies. In general, sawflies are pretty inconspicuous insects, but the Blue Horntail gets its share of attention. The adults are big, heavy-bodied and weird-looking, and the females have a pointed ovipositor that makes them look even more fearsome. Fortunately, they are not dangerous, and the ovipositor is not a sting. Instead, it is used to drill into the wood of trees, where the female lays her eggs, one at a time. The larvae are wood-borers, and some of the horntails are considered pests in some places. When the Blue Horntail gets into lumber, the tunnels of the larvae are conspicuous and difficult to hide. It is a general rule that the larvae of insects that go through a pupa stage are larger and heavier than the adults, because the

LENGTH: 30 mm.
RANGE: throughout Alberta.

transformation from one form to the other is accomplished without the intake of any food. Thus, horntail larvae are larger than horntails, just as caterpillars are larger-bodied than the butterflies and moths that they turn into. Blue Horntails are strongly tied to trees, so they are found only in the forested areas of the province and most commonly in the foothills and the northern boreal forest. There are about six species of horntails in Alberta.

BALD-FACED HORNET

Vespula maculata

If they didn't sting so much, these hornets would be some of our most watchable bugs. They live in colonies, like honey bees, and they build huge paper nests, usually high in the branches of trees. To make the paper, they chew on bark or wood, and mix the pulp with saliva. Then, they add each mouthful to the nest, forming either six-sided cells, where the larvae are reared, or the multi-layered outside cover of the nest. Because each load of pulp comes from a different source, you can see a subtle pattern of grey bands in the paper of the nest. If they are coming to your fence or lawn furniture for pulp, you will soon notice a series of shallow grooves where they have chewed. For food, they visit flowers, catch bugs, and are also attracted to fallen fruit and dead meat. By the time late summer rolls around, the nests are as big as basketballs, and the hornets are ready to defend them at the slightest provocation. In the fall, the colony breaks down, and only the new queens survive the winter, to start new colonies in the spring. The nests don't last long once the leaves fall—birds pick them apart. The Bald-faced Hornet is the largest of three black-and-white "hornets" in Alberta.

LENGTH: about 13 mm.
RANGE: throughout Alberta.

YELLOW JACKET

Vespula spp.

Yellow Jackets are simply smaller versions of the Bald-faced Hornet (p. 82), with yellow markings instead of white. It's too bad we can't just call them all by the same name—it does confuse people when the names "hornet," "wasp" and "jacket" are used interchangeably. It's a good example of a situation where the scientific names make more sense than the English ones (in scientific terms they are all species of *Vespula*). Some Yellow Jackets nest in trees like Bald-faced Hornets do, while others make their paper nests in old rodent burrows in the ground. This type of nesting makes them difficult to spot at a distance, and it is always a shock when you are walking

LENGTH: about 10–15 mm.
RANGE: throughout Alberta.

through the bush and suddenly dozens of angry Yellow Jackets come swarming out of a hidden opening in the earth. You can't blame them—often the nests are discovered by black bears, and the bears tolerate hundreds of stings while they dig up the nest and devour everything inside of it. Yellow Jackets, unlike honey bees, can sting repeatedly although they do eventually run out of venom, I suppose. There are eight species of Yellow Jackets in Alberta.

PAPER WASP

Polistes fuscatus

The name "Paper Wasp" really should go to the Yellow Jacket (p. 83) and the Bald-faced Hornet (p. 82). The "real" Paper Wasp is an amateur by comparison. Its nest is constructed beneath an overhang of some sort, and it has no outside covering. The single layer of paper cells is open to the air, and these wasps never build a second or a third layer. Still, it is interesting to watch Paper Wasps at the nest, because you can actually see what they are doing—something that can't be said of Yellow Jackets or Bald-faced Hornets. The colonies of Paper Wasps are of moderate size, to match the moderate size of their nests. These wasps feed at flowers, especially goldenrod, and they also hunt insects for food. They have painful stings, but our local species is not a particularly defensive one, so few people get stung despite how common the wasps are. To most people, this species is what a "wasp" should look like—long and slender, with a tiny "waist" and narrow wings. To discover that there are thousands of other insects called wasps, many of which are tiny and compact, and most of which are not even social, is a shock to most newcomers to entomology. There is only one species of *Polistes* Paper Wasp in Alberta, but a few other wasps resemble it in shape and colour.

LENGTH: about 18 mm.
RANGE: only in southeastern Alberta.

STUMP STABBER
Family Ichneumonidae, Subfamily Pimplinae

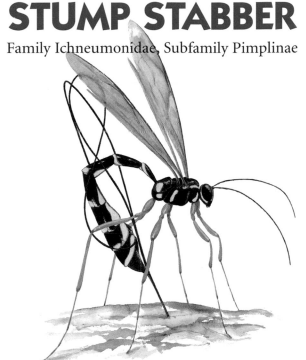

Talk to foresters about bugs and a few familiar species will come up time and again: metallic wood-boring beetles, long-horned beetles, horntails and ichneumons. A big female ichneumon (pronounced *ick-NEW-monn*) can be 85 mm long, including her immense ovipositor—five species can be considered "giant" in Alberta. These bugs looks like something that could definitely hurt you. In fact, many people think they do sting, despite the assurances of entomologists to the contrary. If you find one, follow it. A Stump Stabber flies from tree trunk to tree trunk, all the while rapidly drumming its antennae while running around on the bark, quite obviously searching for something. Then, she stops. Somehow, she has detected a wood-boring grub deep in the wood.

LENGTH: with ovipositor, up to 85 mm.
RANGE: forested regions with coniferous trees.

At this point, she brings her ovipositor to bear, like some sort of strange miniature oil rig. The insect strains to work the tool into the wood, and eventually she finds the larva and forces a slender, very compressible egg down the tube and into the body of her host. There, the egg will hatch and the Stump Stabber grub will proceed to devour its victim from the inside out, leaving its essential organs to the last.

85

THREAD-WAISTED WASP

Ammophila spp.

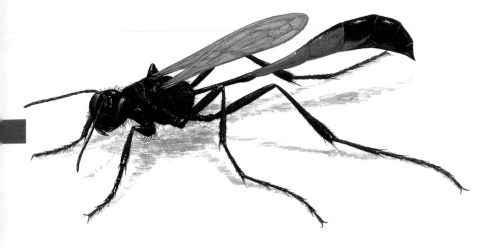

Most wasps are solitary, not colonial. The Thread-waisted Wasp—there are about 12 species in Alberta—is a member of the digger wasp family, and it has fascinating habits. The females sometimes take nectar from flowers, but for the most part they spend their days looking for caterpillars. Once they find one, they sting it in the nerve cord, and inject a paralyzing poison. The caterpillar is then immobilized but still alive. With immense power and determination, the wasp then carries the caterpillar back to a burrow, which she prepared some time before. She opens the burrow, drags the caterpillar down into the dark, and lays an egg on it. Then she comes back to the surface and closes the entrance, sometimes smoothing it over with a pebble held in her jaws. She then goes off to look for another caterpillar, or to dig another burrow. Meanwhile, the egg hatches, and the wasp grub devours the body of the zombie caterpillar. That is, unless some other insect, such as a velvet ant or a parasitic fly, gets its egg into the burrow before it is closed. Then, the invader kills the baby wasp and eats the caterpillar itself.

LENGTH: up to 30 mm.
RANGE: throughout Alberta.

86

SPIDER WASP

Family Pompliidae

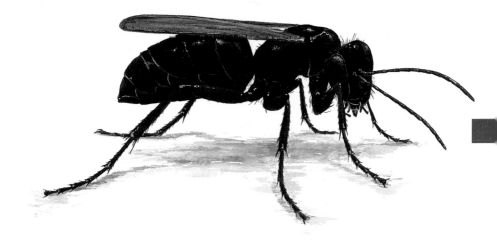

Spider Wasps resemble digger wasps in both form and habits, but they specialize in paralyzing spiders. In fact, they form a separate but related family within the overall category of "hunting wasps." Usually, they are black in colour, at least partially, and many of them have shiny, iridescent blue-black wings. The most famous member of the family is the giant tarantula hawk that lives in the deserts of the American Southwest. Naturalists have long been fascinated by the way these huge, fearless wasps search out tarantula spiders many times their own body weight, and then deftly avoid the spider's great terrible fangs while maneuvering into position to deliver

LENGTH: 10 mm.
RANGE: throughout Alberta.

a paralyzing sting. After that, the story is much the same as for most other hunting wasps, complete with burrow in the ground and a single egg. For our Alberta species (there are about 50 in Alberta), the same dramatic story holds true, but the wasps are so small that no one notices them, and the spiders that fall prey to their macabre rituals are less imposing than a huge tarantula, at least to us. Still, if you get the chance to watch them, any of the hunting wasps can provide hours of good bug-watching entertainment.

HOVER FLY

Family Syrphidae

I t is important to learn to recognize Hover Flies—it will improve the quality of your life. Why? Because many of them look like wasps, for protection, and it's good to be able to tell a real wasp from a fake one. Look for long antennae and a cylindrical abdomen—that's a wasp. If you see tiny antennae and a flattened abdomen—that's a Hover Fly. But be careful, because some Hover Flies wave their front legs as if they were antennae! Hover Flies don't sting, and they don't bite either. In England, there are many people whose hobby is the study of Hover Flies, and there they enjoy the luxury of being able to buy colour field guides to their local species. Perhaps some day we will reach the same level of sophistication here, but for the moment just

LENGTH: about 10 mm.
RANGE: throughout Alberta.

recognizing Hover Flies at all is a good thing. (There are at least 160 species of Hover Flies in Alberta.) It is also important to appreciate how many Hover Flies are involved in the pollination of flowers, because they visit blossoms the same way bees do. The larvae of Hover Flies are interesting, too. Some larvae are predators that feed on aphids, while others are the famous "rat-tailed maggots" that live in the muck at the bottom of shallow ponds.

HORSE FLY

Hybomitra spp.

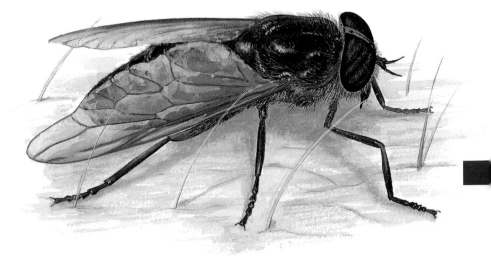

So what could be interesting about a Horse Fly? Well, how about the colours in its eyes? If you get a close-up look at one—perhaps after a lucky swat—check out the eyes and the intense rainbows that enliven the fly's otherwise evil-looking face. These flies feed on blood, and they are most common near lakes. Go for a swim in mid-summer, and I guarantee that by the time you have dried yourself off you will have taken at least one swing at a Horse Fly. They are attracted to large mammals (such as ourselves), and the thing they look for is a dark object with a light spot on it where the sun forms a reflective "highlight." If you drive a black car or a black van, you will find even more of them when you get back to the parking lot. One good thing about Horse Flies is that they are so big, it's hard for one to bite without you knowing it is there. As well, Horse Flies have large blades in their mouthparts, rather than sophisticated slender stylets, like a mosquito. There may be as many as 30 species of Horse Flies in Alberta. A smaller version of a Horse Fly, with dark markings on its wings, is called a Deer Fly (*Chrysops* spp.). In northern Alberta, I've heard Horse Flies called "bull dogs" and Deer Flies called "bull pups."

LENGTH: about 15 mm.
RANGE: throughout Alberta.

BEEISH ROBBER FLY

Laphria spp.

R obber flies don't really steal things, other than life itself. They are amazingly agile predators, and they kill by catching other insects in mid-air. Between hunts, they find a perch on the ground or on vegetation, and from there they scan for potential victims. With large compound eyes, they have excellent vision and an amazing ability not only to spot their prey, but also to follow it through the air in high-speed pursuit. When they catch something, they return to the ground, with their fearsome proboscis deep in the tissues of their unlucky prey. They are not too distantly related to Horse Flies (p. 89), and they have similar sorts of mouthparts. Even beetles can fall prey to robber flies; these flies have perfected the perfect way to kill these heavily armoured insects. While the beetle is flying, its wing covers are spread, exposing the soft abdomen underneath. The robber fly sinks its mouthparts into the beetle's soft spot while the two are still in the air. Most robber flies are not mimics, but the Beeish Robber Fly looks so much like a bumblebee (p. 80) that it is tough to tell the two apart from a distance. There are about 15 species of bee-mimicking robber flies in Alberta.

LENGTH: about 20 mm.
RANGE: throughout Alberta.

GIANT CRANE FLY

Tipula spp.

"Aaaaaggh! A monster mosquito!" That's what most people say the first time they see a Giant Crane Fly, an event which usually occurs while the fly is resting on the foundation of a suburban house. There are many species of crane flies, but the giant ones are large and orange in colour, and they have a pointy tip to the female's abdomen. They look evil, but the truth is you couldn't ask for a nicer bug. These flies don't bite at all, they are actually sort of attractive, and even the larvae are unobtrusive, living as scavengers in the soil. Some people also call these flies "daddy long-legs," a term that is most often used in Alberta to refer to Harvestmen (p. 140), which are a sort of arachnid. In general then, we are surrounded by confusion with respect to Giant Crane Flies, and hopefully this book will lead the way to dispelling our ignorance. Another frequent twist to the finding-one-in-your-garden story is the fact that they are often discovered while mating, end to end. When a mating pair is disturbed, the sight of two sets of wispy flailing wings, 12 immense dangling legs and two giant

LENGTH: up to 25 mm.
RANGE: throughout Alberta.

"mosquitoes" tugging in opposite directions make for a spectacle that is, let's just say, "creepy" to all but the most devoted bugsters among us. There are at least 30 species of Giant Crane Flies in Alberta.

SAND DUNE BEE FLY

Poecilanthrax willistoni

Bee flies look like delta-winged fighter planes, but they are neither fighters nor beeish by nature. You can generally recognize members of this family by their swept-back, dark-coloured wings, and the Sand Dune Bee Fly also has a distinctive pattern that separates it from the others. Many species have clear wings, and some of these are easy to confuse with Hover Flies (p. 88). There are at least 40 species of dark-winged bee flies in Alberta. The Sand Dune Bee Fly, true to its name, is found mainly on bare sand, in the company of both tiger beetles and digger wasps. This location is not a coincidence. The larvae of bee flies are parasitic maggots. Some larvae are parasites of tiger beetle larvae, while others eat the paralyzed insects inside wasp burrows or the larvae of digger bees and wasps themselves. For many, including the Sand Dune Bee Fly, we really don't know what their "hosts" are, because no one has ever studied the matter. It seems odd, when you think of how easy it is to watch these flies, but even if you saw them flying above a tiger beetle or a wasp burrow, flicking eggs into the opening, you couldn't say for sure what their intention was. After all, they will also flick eggs into the lace holes of your shoes.

LENGTH: about 12 mm.
RANGE: throughout Alberta.

SNOW CRANEFLY

Chionea nivalis

There is something odd about bugs that you find on snow. Snow Fleas are the most common, followed by all sorts of bugs that wind up on the snow by accident when they become active on a warm winter's day. The Snow Cranefly, however, is perfectly at home on the "white stuff," although it does require warm days to be active. It uses its long legs to stiffly transport itself across the frozen expanses, and it walks so slowly that you can clearly see how an insect uses its six legs. First, one set of three is put forward, like a tripod, followed by the other set of three. The long legs also hold the body at the correct height—too high and the air would chill the fly, too low and the snow would do the same. These craneflies don't need wings, so they don't have any. In winter, wings only get a bug into trouble. As well, Snow Craneflies are dark in colour to help them warm up in the sun. All of these features make the Snow Cranefly one amazingly well-adapted animal. There are one or two species of Snow Craneflies in Alberta. In the mountains, you might also find the wingless Snow Scorpionfly (*Boreus* spp.), with a long head and a downward-pointed beak.

LENGTH: about 3 mm; leg span about 10 mm.
RANGE: the wooded parts of Alberta.

GREEN LACEWING

Chrysopa spp.

Beautiful, smelly and mean—that's how I think of lacewings. These bugs are familiar garden bugs, and the adults are truly elegant with their many-veined wings, their delicate lime green bodies and their bulging golden eyes. The scientific name *Chrysopa* means exactly that: "golden eyes." Catch one, however, and you will soon notice a truly weird smell as it twists and turns in your fingers, as you hold it by the wings. The smell is a bit like coffee, but not really. In regards to the mean-spirited aspect of their nature, lacewings are predators, and they mostly eat aphids. Thus, they join ladybugs and the larvae of some Hover Flies (p. 88) in a "friends of the gardener" category, despite the fact that none of them even know what a gardener is. Young lacewings, which are larvae much like those of a ladybug,

LENGTH: about 10 mm.
RANGE: throughout Alberta.

are also aphid eaters. They are so vicious that the mother lacewing lays each egg on the top of a long, slender stalk, so the first larva to hatch doesn't eat all of its brothers and sisters before they can get out of the egg. There are four or so species of lacewings in Alberta. As well as the green ones, watch for Brown Lacewings. There are even blotchy ones, usually early and late in the season.

SNAP-TRAP ANT LION

Brachynemurus abdominalis

An adult ant lion is a gangly creature. It looks like a dull coloured damselfly, but up close it is more like a stretched-out Brown Lacewing (p. 94), with large antennae where a damselfly would have tiny ones. It is, however, the larvae of the ant lion that attract attention, with their habit of building conical pits in the dust. They bury themselves at the bottom and wait until an ant, or other small bug, tumbles over the edge. Then they flick sand and dirt at the intended prey, forcing it to slip further down into the "pit of despair." When it hits the bottom, the larva's jaws close, piercing the cuticle of the victim and sucking it dry through the hollow hypodermic mandibles. In Alberta, these pit-building sorts of ant lions are not very common, and they are found only along the southern border. Elsewhere, in sandy areas, one finds the Snap-trap Ant Lion, whose larvae do not dig pits. Instead, they lie just below the surface of the sand, with the tips of their jaws protruding. Like an old-fashioned snap trap hidden on a rabbit trail, they wait with amazing patience until just the right bug steps in just the right place. There are at least two species of ant lions in Alberta.

LENGTH: adults up to 25 mm.
RANGE: the southern two-thirds of Alberta.

WESTERN OKANAGAN CICADA

Okanagana occidentalis

I n some parts of North America, cicadas are a big deal, especially when they emerge by the millions, cover the trunks of trees, and drown out all other sounds with their incredibly loud buzzing. The larvae of these big insects live for years by underground feeding on roots, and they emerge in early summer. Here in Alberta, however, most people don't even know they exist, even though there are at least six species of cicadas. To find one, you first have to learn what they sound like—a prolonged, dry, rattling buzz. That's the male, and he sits on a slender tree branch while singing, often three or more metres above the ground. If you are very stealthy, you might be able to get close enough to spot him. One false move, however, and he will either fly away or go silent on you. The sound is produced by a vibrating mechanism in the abdomen, a resonating chamber and a thin membrane something like a banjo skin. For its size, a cicada can be incredibly noisy. Looking for cicadas will also introduce you to the Clay-coloured Sparrow. When I was young, I called them "Cicada Birds" because they sounded so much like a cicada, down low in the grass—where cicadas seldom dwell.

LENGTH: about 22 mm.
RANGE: throughout the wooded parts of Alberta.

96

BOX ELDER BUG

Boisea trivittatus

In Alberta, this one is almost always called a "Maple Bug," and I know that many people will criticize me for using its official name instead. It is true, however, that these bugs feed mainly on the seeds of the Manitoba maple tree. In other parts of the continent, this tree is called the "Box Elder," hence the bug is, too. Most people don't like the Box Elder Bug, mind you, because it has a habit of congregating in houses to spend winter. When the family is gathering around the table for New Year's dinner, and a big clumsy Box Elder Bug goes buzzing across the room, bangs into the chandelier, and lands in the mashed potatoes, who can blame anyone for taking offense? It is important, at these moments, to remember that they don't do any harm, and that up close they are actually quite handsome. These bugs are easy to identify here. Bugsters will immediately recognize the function of their black and red colours—to warn predators that they taste bad (even though they don't smell bad). When they are young, they are even more colourful, more red than black. It is only when they get their wings, as adults, that the mainly black wings cover the bright red abdomen.

LENGTH: about 12 mm.
RANGE: in the southern part of Alberta, but not in the foothills or mountains.

97

BIG GREEN STINK BUG

Chlorochroa sayi

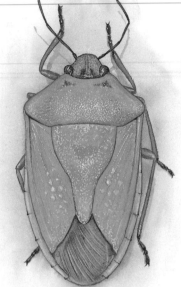

S tink bugs stink. They do so with scent glands that produce a chemical with an odour unlike anything else that you or I are likely to ever encounter. This odour makes them easy to recognize up close, but they are also obvious in other ways. Stink bugs have broad, pointed shoulders and a large, triangular plate in the middle of their back (the scutellum, for those of you who like to know these things). Some stink bugs are more triangular than others, so if in doubt, sniff. Some feed on other insects, while others suck the juices from plants and plant seeds. There are many stink bugs in Alberta, but only two huge, green ones. The Big Green Stink Bug is one of our biggest with a lovely green colour. The Uhler's Stink Bug (*C. uhleri*) is about the same size and colour, and it feeds on juniper shrubs—mainly Alberta's wild creeping juniper. Stink bugs are also known for their prowess as devoted mothers. They lay a cluster of intricately sculptured eggs, all together on the surface of a leaf. Then the mother guards the brood until they hatch, at which point the babies are free to fend for themselves. Baby stink bugs, like all sucking bugs, are much like tiny adults but without wings.

LENGTH: about 12 mm.
RANGE: the southern half of Alberta.

AMBUSH BUG

Phymata erosa

S mall but dangerous, that's an Ambush Bug. It isn't dangerous to people, mind you, but to any sort of insect that visits flowers it is trouble incarnate. In the same fashion as a Goldenrod Crab Spider (p. 150), an Ambush Bug lies in wait for unwary pollinators, sometimes tucking in deep among the flower parts in order to stay well hidden. Our single Ambush Bug species is a yellowish colour, with large angular flanges on the sides of its abdomen that may help break up its outline and enhance the ambush effect. Ambush Bugs have strong middle and rear legs that they use to hold tight to the flowers. Their front legs, on the other hand, are enormously strong for their

LENGTH: about 9 mm.
RANGE: only in the prairies of southeastern Alberta.

size. With them an Ambush Bug can subdue even gigantic bumblebees or butterflies many times its own size. Then, in the fashion typical of predatory bugs, it injects a digestive fluid into its prey, waits for the insides of the insect to soften, and then sucks the insides from its victims. I have seen these insects mainly in the latter part of the summer, when they are easiest to find among the flowers of goldenrod plants.

WEE HARLEQUIN BUG
Cosmopepla bimaculata

A lthough it is small, this insect is one of our most colourful, with bold black, yellow and red markings and a glossy shine to boot. Wee Harlequin Bugs turn up quite often in gardens, as well, which makes them a favourite of the bugster crowd. If you try to identify them with the usual North American field guides, however, the closest you will come is to something called a "Harlequin Bug." Our species is about half the size, so I call it the Wee Harlequin Bug, mainly because I like the word "wee" better than "small" or "lesser"—the usual word in most animal names. This bug is a member of the stink bug family, but it is less robust than Say's or Uhler's stink bugs. Still, it stinks, although perhaps a bit less than some of its relatives. Wee Harlequin Bugs feed on a variety of plants, including oats, mint and goldenrod, and they are therefore widely distributed across Canada and the United States. As well, the adults are relatively long lived, so you can find them all through the bug season. I like a bug that sticks around for a while and lets you get to know it, and I like one that fearlessly sits in the open as well.

LENGTH: about 5 mm.
RANGE: throughout Alberta.

SUPERB PLANT BUG

Adelphocoris superbus

The plant bug family is a big one, but this species stands out from the rest of the crowd. It is beautifully coloured in red and black, and at a distance you might even mistake it for a ladybug (pp. 71–73). It has the criss-crossed, leathery front wings of a sucking bug, however, not the hard-

LENGTH: 8 mm.
RANGE: the southeastern corner of Alberta.

ened wing covers of a beetle. Remember, ladybugs are beetles. If you look at the Superb Plant Bug with a magnifying glass, you'll see another neat thing—a perfect little red Valentine heart in the middle of its back! Now what could it be doing with that? Technically, the heart-shaped part is the scutellum, the same piece that is big and triangular on a stink bug. The fact that it is exactly the same shape and colour as a cartoon heart may seem like a weird coincidence to some people, but really what it tells us is something about the diversity of bugs. There are so many bugs, with so many different shapes and colours that if you look long enough you can find almost any shape you want. For example, one clever insect photographer found all the letters of the alphabet, along with the numbers 1 through 10, in the patterns on butterfly and moth wings.

NORTHERN ROCK CRAWLER

Grylloblatta campodeiformis

To find this amazing wingless insect, one has to venture high into the mountains and search among the rocky talus slopes up above treeline. Our province holds a special place in the story of the Northern Rock Crawler, because it was here that it was first discovered. In 1914 Edmund Walker, a Canadian entomologist, described the first Rock Crawlers from Banff National Park, of all places. He realized that he was looking at not only a new species, but also a new genus, a new family and a new order—in other words, a whole new kind of a bug! To entomologists, Rock Crawlers are interesting because they are so "primitive-looking." That means they look like an "average" bug, from which a lot of others could have evolved. To ordinary folks, they have other interesting attributes. For example, if you pick one up and hold it in your hand, the heat from your hulking mammalian body will kill it. That's how well adapted they are to the cool climate of the alpine zone. An adult Rock Crawler is likely to be seven years old, by the way, and it feeds mainly on other insects, especially wingless crane flies.

LENGTH: up to 30 mm.
RANGE: high in the mountains.

FIELD CRICKET

Gryllus veletis

There is no more classic sound of summer than the chirping of crickets. Actually seeing a cricket chirp, on the other hand, is no easy matter. If you do manage to get a peek, you'll find that only the males make sounds. (Males have two pointy things—the cerci—out the back of their abdomen, while females have three—two cerci and one egg-laying ovipositor). To make the sound, male crickets rub their two wing covers together, like bringing a rasp into contact with a file. The hardened wing covers amplify and resonate to produce the noise we all know and love. As for the old Boy Scout trick of counting the number of chirps per minute and using it to calculate the temperature (because they chirp more slowly in the cold), think about this: there are five species of crickets in Alberta, and each one chirps at a dif-

LENGTH: about 20 mm.
RANGE: the southern half of Alberta.

ferent rate. So first you need to know the species you are listening to. Then, remember that the Boy Scout formula was calculated with tree crickets in the East, meaning we need all-new formulae for Alberta's field crickets. If it all seems like more trouble than carrying a small thermometer, consider yourself normal.

103

CAVE CRICKET

Ceuthophilus spp.

I n some parts of the world, Cave Crickets actually hang out in caves. Here in Alberta, however, they live mostly in rodent burrows, under rocks and logs and in rotten wood. What they want is a place that is moist and dark. For those of you who think *Homo sapiens* has advanced beyond the "caveman" stage, all I can say is go look in your basement. There, on occasion, you will find a Cave Cricket or two, but only if you are lucky. They need access to water, and they are usually found somewhere near the floor drain. Don't let them worry you, because they do no harm. Some people mistake them for cockroaches, but roaches are much flatter and faster, and do not have jumping hindlegs. Another name for Cave Crickets is "Camel Crickets," based on their hump-backed shape. Note as well that they have no wings, and therefore cannot chirp like other crickets. There are six species of Cave Crickets in Alberta, all of which have very long antennae.

LENGTH: about 12 mm.
RANGE: the southern half of Alberta and the Peace River area.

The true cave dwellers, found elsewhere, have even longer feelers, as well as elongate legs. There is a painting of a Cave Cricket among the famous cave paintings of France. At 16,000 years old, it is the oldest depiction on an insect that has ever been discovered. As they say: *Plus ça change, plus c'est la même chose.* (The more things change, the more they stay the same!)

ROAD DUSTER

Dissosteira carolina

This species, which is also called the "Carolina Locust," is the signature grasshopper of vacant lots, construction sites, railway lines and gravel pits. In flight, this remarkable hopper looks like a Mourning Cloak butterfly (p. 36), with black hindwings and a narrow, white border. As a young bug fanatic, I was fooled more than once by this resemblance. Recently, some entomologists have suggested that various band-winged grasshoppers (the subgroup to which the Road Duster belongs) resemble butterflies for a reason. The patterns on some butterflies may advertise to birds that the butterfly is a super-fast flyer that is not worth pursuing, and the grasshoppers may gain some protection by mimicking these butterflies' patterns. The Road Duster is the only grasshopper in Alberta with black hindwings. Some other band-winged grasshoppers resemble sulphur butterflies (p. 29). The Road Duster's main defence when in flight is to simply drop to the ground and

LENGTH: 30–40 mm.
RANGE: the southern two-thirds of Alberta.

fold the wings. While on the ground, it is extremely difficult to see, what with its cinnamon brown–grey body. It is so much like a dirt lump that even its eyes blend with the colour of the rest of the head. Male Road Dusters do an interesting courtship display called "the hover flight." Watch for one to hover in mid-air, about 1 m above the ground, fluttering his wings softly, first quickly and then at a slower speed.

RED-WINGED CLICKHOPPER

Arphia conspersa

Unlike most butterfly-like, band-winged grasshoppers, the Red-winged Clickhopper doesn't actually resemble any particular butterfly. This one has bright red hindwings with a black border. There are five species of red-winged grasshoppers in Alberta. Many other species are yellow with a black border—the ones that are supposed to look like sulphur butterflies. Our biggest yellow-winged grasshopper, the Red-shanked Grasshopper (*Xanthippus corallipes*), may be the biggest adult insect in Alberta—heavy and up to 41 mm long. Perhaps the Red-winged Clickhopper resembles some sort of red-and-black butterfly that is now extinct, or perhaps to a bird the difference between red-and-black and yellow-and-black is not such a big deal. When I am out on spring butterfly walks, there are plenty of false-alarm moments when people mistake a Clickhopper for a butterfly that "landed here, in the grass someplace."

LENGTH: about 25 mm.
RANGE: throughout Alberta.

Speaking of springtime, farmers and gardeners are used to thinking of grasshoppers spending the winter as eggs, and becoming numerous only in the latter part of the summer. The Red-winged Clickhopper, in contrast, spends the winter almost, but not quite, fully grown, and it moults to become an adult in early spring.

GIANT STONEFLY

Pteronarcys californica

Adult Giant Stoneflies are encountered frequently by people walking near rivers. When you least expect it, there is suddenly a huge, flattened insect crawling on your clothes in a frenzied and highly unnerving manner. Of course, like most bugs, it can't, and doesn't want to, harm you. Still, it is in this manner that most people are introduced to stoneflies. Another way that many people get to know this group is by reading dinosaur books. When you look at the paintings of the amphibians and reptiles that "ruled the earth" before the dinosaurs, there are often stoneflies added by the artist, along with other ancient sorts of bugs, such as dragonflies and cockroaches. Leaving aside the fact that we all know that bugs, not dinosaurs, have always ruled the earth, it is interesting that stoneflies have remained more-or-less unchanged for about 300 million years. They are also interesting to watch in the here and now, especially when they drum their abdomens on the stems of plants, as a courtship signal to the opposite sex. In flight, however, they are a far cry from masters of the air, proving that for almost a third of a billion years, it really didn't matter. There are about six really large species of stoneflies in Alberta.

LENGTH: 40 mm, including the folded wings.
RANGE: common along rivers and streams.

GERMAN COCKROACH

Blatta germanica

It is unfortunate for the German people that this cockroach is named in their country's honour. It is also unfortunate for the many thousands of harmless woodland cockroaches, living in the tropics around the world, that we temperate folks get such a poor introduction to their diversity and splendour. Of course, the cockroaches we find in this part of the world are all introduced, and they are all capable of "infesting" houses and other buildings. They seem to especially like greenhouses. Once under a safe roof, they feed on just about anything edible, although they do need water, which they get from condensation or from water traps and drain-pipes. They are active after dark and very difficult to catch. Their cerci (the two feelers on the end of the abdomen) can detect even the slightest breezes, and cockroaches instantly run when they feel

LENGTH: about 15 mm.
RANGE: potentially anywhere in Alberta.

the pressure wave of an approaching foot. Cockroaches are very rarely implicated in the spread of disease, despite what you might hear. Generally, they are most abundant in places where things are most messy, and in those sorts of environments diseases have no problem getting around by themselves. There are perhaps six species of cockroaches in Alberta.

BOREAL BLUET

Enallagma boreale

If you have ever spent time beside a pond or a lake in June, you have seen these bluer-than-blue bugs. Like phosphorescent toothpicks, they hover among the reeds, where they catch their prey by plucking it off leaves while in flight. Aphids and baby grasshoppers are about the right size for a damselfly to tackle—yes, Boreal Bluets are a type of damselfly. More specifically, they are a type of American bluet (in the genus *Enallagma*). The males are patterned in blue and black, while some females are green or yellow, instead of blue. Unfortunately, our seven species of American bluets all look more-or-less exactly alike. In cases like this, entomology books usually say something like "identification is best left to specialists." In reality, it's not that hard. All you need is a good magnifying glass and some obscure information. More and more, damselfly and dragonfly watching is catching up in popularity to butterfly watching, which in turn is slowly catching up to bird watching. If you've tried bird watching, and if you believe that mere mortals can actually identify sparrows and shorebirds in the field, then you may some day agree that the bluets are manageable, too. There are seven species of American bluets in Alberta.

LENGTH: 32 mm.
RANGE: throughout Alberta.

TAIGA BLUET

Coenagrion resolutum

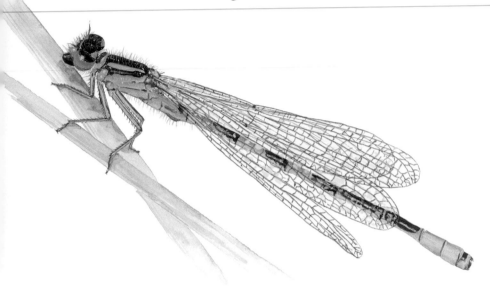

The lovely male Taiga Bluet is blue on top and green underneath. Not only is that a vibrant colour combination, it also helps separate male Eurasian bluets from male American bluets (p. 109). Females are more difficult to tell apart, at least for people, but the damselflies themselves have an interesting way of sorting each other out. On the tip of the male's abdomen are a set of claspers that fit perfectly on the back the female's neck. When a male tries to mate with a female, he first attempts to get her in a headlock, so to speak. At this point, three things can happen. First, he can succeed, after which they fly away in tandem, mate and deposit the eggs. Second, the female may reject the male and evade his claspers with a bit of damselfly judo. Third, the male may find that his claspers don't quite fit, which may be a sign that he has accosted the wrong species of female, or worse, another male. There are three Eurasian bluets in Alberta, but only two are commonly seen. Look for Taiga Bluets mostly in June. The American bluets seem to last much longer into summer in most places.

LENGTH: 30 mm.
RANGE: throughout Alberta.

COMMON SPREADWING

Lestes disjunctus

These damselflies have only a bit of blue on them, right at the tip of the abdomen and again at the base of the wings. When they are young, they are iridescent green or brown, and as they get older they become covered in a waxy powder, like the "bloom" on a plum. Together, damselflies and dragonflies form the insect order Odonata. Unfortunately, we have no word in English that refers to them both together. British people use the word "dragonfly" in this way, but it seems to me that giving "dragonfly" two confusingly similar meanings is a bad idea. I prefer the term "odonates" or just simply "odes" myself. Telling damselflies from dragonflies is easy: damselflies are thin, and all of their wings are similar in shape; dragonflies are more heavily built, and the hindwings are broader than the fore-

LENGTH: 35 mm.
RANGE: the southern two-thirds of Alberta.

wings. Some people will tell you that damselflies always fold their wings over their backs, but obviously the spreadwings are an exception to this rule. Almost all the damselflies in Alberta are spreadwings, American bluets or Eurasion bluets, and the rest are all rare and hard to find. Alberta's four species of spreadwing damselflies are most common later in the summer.

VARIABLE DARNER

Aeshna interrupta

LENGTH: 70 mm.
RANGE: throughout Alberta.

The darners are our biggest dragonflies, and the Variable Darner is the most common of the lot. Up close, the male is a dark brown insect, patterned in blue and green. Some of the females are coloured this way, while others are brown and yellow. Thus, they are variable. Darners spend most of the day on the wing, cruising the mid-summer skies for insects, which they capture in flight with their long, spiny legs. In turn, the darners are an important source of food for Merlin falcons, and young Merlins learn their hunting skills by chasing darners through the air. Darners breed in ponds and lakes, but they will also wander far from water to feed. The name "darner," by the way, comes from the mistaken notion that these dragonflies will sew up your lips with their stinger. In reality, they have no stinger, and they don't sew, so put aside your fears. Some entomologists have suggested that this rumour got started when people wading in the shallows were accidentally jabbed by female darners, trying to lay eggs. I guess a bare leg is easy to mistake for a soft water plant. There are 12 species of darners in Alberta, and they are on the wing from late June until the killing frosts of October.

PALE SNAKETAIL

Ophiogomphus severus

Most dragonflies live near ponds and lakes, because that is where their larvae grow up. The snaketails, however, and other members of the clubtail family, have larvae that also live in rivers and streams. The adults are rarely common, and for dragonfly experts they are always a thrill to see. Watch for a pale dragonfly that sits on the ground between flights.

Up close, notice that the eyes of these dragonflies are widely separated, rather than meeting in the middle of the head. Although the clubtail family is named for the expanded abdomen tips of some of its members, the snake-tails have only a modest "club." The Pale Snaketail is easy to find along the valleys of the bigger rivers in mid-summer. Notice that its coloration includes none of the intense blues and reds of other dragonflies. Instead, it is a light grass green. Green colour in animals is typically produced by a combination of yellow pigment and a blue "scattering" of light—the same thing that makes the sky blue. In other words, "Why is the sky blue?" is a much simpler question with the same answer as "Why is the snaketail green?" There are four dragonfly species in the clubtail family in Alberta.

LENGTH: 50 mm.
RANGE: throughout Alberta.

AMERICAN EMERALD

Cordulia shurtleffi

What a fine dragonfly! With gleaming, green eyes and a jade-black, iridescent body, it has a certain style all its own. The American Emerald, our most common member of the emerald family, is a dragonfly of the early summer. It lays its eggs in ponds and small lakes, which is probably why it is so common. Other sorts of emeralds prefer boggy pools deep in black spruce and tamarack peatlands or high mountain lakes, which contributes not only to their rarity but also to their appeal. It's hard to say whether emeralds or clubtails generate more excitement among dragonfly enthusiasts, but it's probably a safe bet that clubtails rule in the south, while emeralds are symbols of the great northern forests. To get a good look at any of the 11 species of emeralds in Alberta, it really does help to catch them. Crouching by a skinny little brook flowing through the muskeg below a beaver pond, the "odonatist" waits. Mosquitoes swarm by the dozens, but the stalker dares not swat them for fear of spooking a passing dragonfly. When one finally comes in reach, one swing of the net is all it will allow, and with it you either bag the emerald or you do not.

LENGTH: 45 mm.
RANGE: throughout the forested areas of Alberta.

HUDSONIAN WHITEFACE

Leucorrhinia hudsonica

This dragonfly is one of the first to emerge in spring. In warm years that means May, but when the weather is cool the first ones may not pop out until June. The whiteface dragonflies are recognizable by their combination of a bright white face and a small, black splotch near the base of each hindwing. The rest of the body is boldly patterned in black and red (on mature males) or black and yellow (on most females and young males). The bright, contrasting colours are further enhanced by a coat of white hairs on the underside of the body. Whitefaces are some of our smallest dragonflies, but they are also among our most beautiful. In contrast to the meadowhawks that emerge later in the year, whitefaces seem to spend more time around the ponds in which they breed. There, they perch on floating logs, scan the newly leafed shorelines for potential mates and sometimes wander out into clearings and along woodsy trails in the process. When the first mosquitoes of the year emerge, whitefaces are their nemeses; of course, these dragonflies eat other insects as well, especially if they are abundant. There are five species of whitefaces in Alberta.

LENGTH: 30 mm.
RANGE: throughout Alberta.

115

FOUR-SPOTTED SKIMMER

Libellula quadrimaculata

The name of this fine dragonfly proves one thing beyond any doubt: entomologists can't count. Because the wings on one side of the body look just like the wings on the other side, I guess they didn't bother counting all eight black spots. If you count the black hindwing bases, there are really 10 spots, but at this point who cares? In any case, this skimmer is a handsome animal, with a thick muscular body and a broad, streamlined abdomen. When it is in the prime of its life, its colours are vivid orange and black, but they do fade as the dragonfly gets older. You mostly see Four-spotted Skimmers around ponds and lakes, and they seem to like patrolling along the reedy shorelines. The females are alone when they lay their eggs, dipping their abdomens in the water while they fly. (Males of many other dragonfly species remain attached to the female so no other male can interrupt the egg-laying process and mate with the female again.) The Four-spotted Skimmer also lives in Europe, where it is famous for mass-migrations that blacken the skies and for coming to rest by the thousands on ocean-going ships. Too bad it doesn't happen in Alberta as well—the migrations that is, not the ocean-going ships. There are three similar-sized but differently coloured "king skimmers" in Alberta.

LENGTH: 42 mm.
RANGE: throughout Alberta.

116

CHERRY-FACED MEADOWHAWK

Sympetrum internum

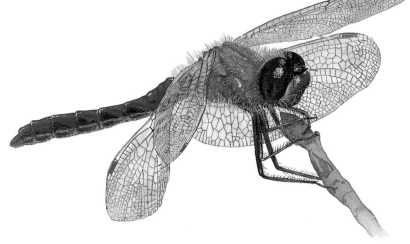

For most Albertans there are two kinds of dragonflies: the big blue ones and the little, red or yellow ones. The blue ones are, of course, the darners, while the red or yellow ones are the meadowhawks. Meadowhawks are about the same size as whitefaces, but they do not have a dark base on the hindwing, and they fly later in the season. The Cherry-faced Meadowhawk is the most common of the eight species that are found in Alberta. Males have a deep red body and a truly cherry red face. Females and young males are yellowish. Unlike whitefaces, meadowhawks wander a great distance from their breeding ponds, and they show up in parks and gardens all the time. They like to perch on the ground or on low vegetation, so you can usually sneak up on them to get a good look.

It was here in Alberta that an unusual aspect of this dragonfly's behaviour was first observed. A visiting bugster

LENGTH: 35 mm.
RANGE: throughout Alberta.

from Europe noticed that pairs of Cherry-faced Meadowhawks would fly low over lawns, dipping the female's abdomen to lay eggs. To the dragonflies, a mowed lawn must look like a place that would flood in the springtime, sure to provide habitat for their aquatic larvae. Some other species can also be fooled into laying eggs on shiny cars!

117

BLACK MEADOWHAWK

Sympetrum danae

True to its name, our second most common meadowhawk is easy to recognize because the males are almost black once they mature. They are the only male meadowhawks with absolutely no red on them. Females and young males are patterned in black and yellow, and they look a lot like female whitefaces. While whitefaces emerge at the beginning of dragonfly season, Black Meadowhawks first appear in mid-summer. They seem to live a long time, and the last dragonfly I see most years, in mid- to late October, is a Black Meadowhawk hugging the ground for warmth while the sun sinks lower and lower in the sky. Like the Four-spotted Skimmer (p. 116), this dragonfly is also found in Europe and northern Asia.

LENGTH: 38 mm.
RANGE: throughout Alberta.

It behaves much like a Cherry-faced Meadowhawk (p. 117), but it is less likely to show up in your garden and less gullible when it comes to laying eggs in lawns. The scientific name, by the way, means "Danae's rock-lover": *sym* means "loving"; *petrum* means "rock"; and when you see a scientific name that ends in *-ae*, it generally refers to a woman's name (*-i* refers to a man's). There are eight species of meadowhawks in Alberta.

SNOW FLEA

Family Isotomuridae

Snow Fleas are really springtails, and springtails are really either very primitive insects or a group of arthropods that are so primitive that they shouldn't be even considered insects. They never have wings, even as adults, and they are all tiny little dwellers in leaf litter and other moist places, where they are scavengers on decaying matter. Most people see Snow Fleas, oddly enough, in winter, when they come out on the snow during the midday warmth of unseasonable Chinook afternoons. With their amazing "tails," they leap about on the surface of the snow, obviously immune to the cold. The tail is actually an organ that comes out of the bottom of the springtail's abdomen, and it is used like a catapult to fling the bug up into the air. Most likely, they are not entirely pleased to be on snow and are trying to get to someplace where the snow has melted, so they can go back to life the way they like it. It is possible, however, that they do find things to eat on the snow—if you have a good close look at the surface of partly melted snow, you'll see it's not as clean as it looks from up high. There are probably a few dozen to a few hundred species of springtails in Alberta.

LENGTH: up to 2 mm.
RANGE: throughout Alberta.

119

KAYAK POND SKATER

Limnoporus dissortis

L et's face it, it's just plain weird that an animal can live on top of the water without falling through. Pond skaters accomplish this feat in a fascinating way. Four very long legs support their slender body, and thus their wispy mass is distributed over a large area of the water's surface. The water itself has a sort of skin to it (the "surface tension") that is strong enough to support an insect, but only if its legs repel water, which naturally a pond skater's do. For these little bugs, the surface of a pond must feel like a great, slippery waterbed mattress stretching off in all directions. On this bizarre playing field, they search for food in the form of other bugs that have fallen in and drowned or are in the process of drowning. Because pond skaters are sucking bugs, they have the same sort of piercing proboscis that allows their aquatic relatives to overpower and consume their own buggy prey. Kayak Pond Skaters have wings, but many of their relatives grow into adults that are wingless. Those pond skaters that are winged can leave the pond and settle elsewhere, while those that are wingless must be satisfied with their humble birthpool and trust that things will remain to their liking. There are six pond skater species in Alberta.

LENGTH: 12 mm.
RANGE: throughout Alberta.

GIANT WATER BUG

Lethocerus americanus

With its swollen forearms, this critter looks a bit like Arnold Schwarz-enegger holding two long spikes in front of his head. Oddly enough, it also looks like a domino-sized piece of wet, brown cardboard. Once a Giant Water Bug grasps a luckless fish, tadpole or fellow insect, the result is inevitable: the sucking beak plunges deep, digestive juices are injected, and the prey dissolves inside its own body. The water bug holds on and waits until the time is right to suck up its meal. When it is done, the water bug swims off to digest its food. This bug has two pairs of swimming legs, not one. After all, it is our largest aquatic insect, and it needs the extra power to propel its hefty body through the water. These impressive creatures, the only one of their kind in Alberta, can be found in still or slow-flowing waters, and they are most abundant in cattail marshes. In flight, they look a lot like a small bat and are often attracted to lights at night. Young Giant Water Bugs look much like adults, but without the wings. And yes, if one bites you, it really does hurt.

LENGTH: 50 mm.
RANGE: throughout Alberta.

AUDEN'S WATER BOATMAN

Callicorixa audeni

Although small, water boatmen are amazing. Just take a look at their legs: the first pair are shaped like little garden trowels, and the bug uses them for sifting through muck for food; the next pair are long and pointed, and the boatman uses them to hold on to plants or rocks while underwater; and then there are the back legs, which are the boatman's oars. If you keep a water boatman in a glass jar, you can see how it breathes under water. When it dives, a layer of air clings to the boatman's tummy. It breathes from this bubble. The oxygen the bug needs enters the bubble from the surrounding water. At the same time, carbon dioxide leaves the bubble and goes into the pond. Slowly, the bubble gets smaller as nitrogen goes into the water, and then the bug pops to the surface to replenish its air supply. The Auden's Water Boatman is the most common of about 30 species in Alberta. It lives both in ponds and rivers. At times, it can gather by the millions in one place, and when they accidentally fly to lights at night, they can cover the ground with their bodies.

LENGTH: 8 mm.
RANGE: throughout Alberta.

COMMON BACKSWIMMER

Notonecta undulata

A re you any good at the backstroke? Well, it seems that the back-swimmer doesn't know any other way to swim. At first, you might think that a backswimmer is just an upside-down water boatman, but have another look. Both its pairs of front legs are short and stocky, for grabbing prey, and instead of resting on underwater plants, backswimmers lounge right at the top of the pond. They rest with their legs touching the underside of the water surface, and their heads aimed slightly down, ready to dive. If you catch one and flip it over, you'll see how pretty it is, with bright white wings and fiery red eyes. Don't let it bite you, though! The bite of a back-swimmer is like that of a Giant Water Bug—intended to dissolve the flesh of their prey. People who keep fish in outdoor ponds dread backswim-mers, because they eat a lot of small fish, as well as other bugs. In nature,

LENGTH: 11 mm.
RANGE: throughout Alberta.

however, backswimmers are both predator and prey, and they make the world of the pond more interesting, even if it is a bit more dangerous. Backswimmers are predators, but they live in fear of such things as Giant Water Bugs (p. 121), Giant Diving Beetles (p. 126) and bigger fish, too. There are four species of backswimmers in Alberta.

ACILIUS DIVING BEETLE

Acilius spp.

LENGTH: 13 mm.
RANGE: throughout Alberta.

Most water bugs and water beetles float, whether they want to or not. When they swim, you can see how they fight to stay down in the water, and how they drift up to the top the moment they quit paddling. Not so with the Acilius Diving Beetle; it seems to be able to match its buoyancy to the water around it. This super-streamlined creature slips through the water like a polished pumpkin seed—it is one of the most graceful swimmers in the insect world. You mostly find these diving beetles in natural ponds, rather than in the sorts of meltwater ponds that form in parks and schoolyards in spring. They are not rare, but they are always exciting to catch. You can recognize them by the half-moon markings on the tips of their wing covers and by the snappy yellow slash on the pronotum shield behind the head. As with the Giant Diving Beetle (p. 126), the male Acilius Diving Beetle has round sucker pads on his front feet to help him hold on to the slippery female while they mate. There are three species of Acilius Diving Beetles in Alberta, plus another three in the closely related group of *Graphoderus* Diving Beetles.

MID-SIZED DIVING BEETLE

Colymbetes sculptilis

About the same size as Acilius Diving Beetles (p. 124), but much more commonly encountered, Mid-sized Diving Beetles fly to meltwater ponds. These beetles don't mind living for a while in places that are nothing more than flooded playgrounds, where they chase down water boatmen and other small bugs and chew them to pieces with their strong jaws. You might even find one on top of a car on a sunny day. To them, a shiny car looks like a small pond, but when they fly down to dive into the water, they suddenly find themselves upside-down on a hot metal roof. Diving beetles have trouble flipping over once they are on their backs, and they also find it tough to take flight on land, so many of them die on hot cars, unable to escape. If you look very closely at a Mid-sized Diving Beetle, you'll see that it is smooth, but that it also has hundreds of very fine lines running crosswise on the tops

LENGTH: 17 mm.
RANGE: throughout Alberta.

of its wing covers, which is a good way to recognize this species. There are four species of Mid-sized Diving Beetles in Alberta. If you find one that looks right but is about half the size, it is probably one of the *Rhantus* Diving Beetles, which are also interesting and also common in meltwater ponds.

GIANT DIVING BEETLE
Dytiscus spp.

N ext to the Giant Water Bug, and some really big dragonfly larvae, Giant Diving Beetles are our biggest aquatic insects. They are power- ful predators that will eat almost anything they can subdue. If you keep pond critters in an aquarium, you will find that sooner or later there is only one left. In most cases the survivor will be either a Giant Water Bug (p. 121) or a Giant Diving Beetle. The Alaskan Diving Beetle (*D. alaskanus*) is probably the most common of the nine species in Alberta, but it is also one of the small- est. The most impressive member of this group is the Harris's Diving Beetle (*D. harrisii*)—a big one can be 40 mm long! In most species, female Giant Diving Beetles come in two forms: the first form looks a lot like a male, with shiny black wing covers; the second form has grooves running the length of the wing covers, making it look at first glance like it must be a different species. A female with a white blob on the end of her abdomen has been mated. The white stuff discourages other males from mating with her again. Males have round sucker pads on their front feet for holding on to the females. If you notice a bad smell when handling one of these beetles, it is probably its defence chemicals—powerful steroids that predators respect.

LENGTH: 27 mm.
RANGE: throughout Alberta.

WHIRLIGIG BEETLE

Gyrinus spp.

Whirligigs are probably the coolest water beetles of them all. With the most efficient swimming legs in the entire animal world, they zip around on top of the water spinning and whirling like super-fast bumper cars. If they need to, they can dive underwater like a diving beetle, and they also have wings when the time comes to find a new pond. Sometimes, dozens of them band together to form a flotilla on the surface. If you have a micro-scope and a whirligig specimen, you can see how amazing its eyes are. Each eye is actually split it two: one half looks up into the air; the other half gazes down into the water! Of course, while they are spinning and whirling at high speed, their eyes need all the help they can get, so they also use their short triangular antennae to "feel" their way through the twists and turns. Whirligig Beetles are predators, and they will eat any unfortunate bug they can catch on the water's surface. Even baby water striders are not fast

LENGTH: 4–6 mm.
RANGE: throughout Alberta.

enough to get away from them. And if another animal tries to eat a Whirligig, it gets a mouthful of something that smells a lot like rotting fruit. There are 12 species of Whirligig Beetles in Alberta

OBTUSE WATER SCAVENGER BEETLE

Hydrochara obtusata

F inally, a water beetle that isn't a ferocious predator. Water scavengers are the gentle members of the water beetle crowd, and they feed on plants and various sorts of debris. When they swim, they paddle like crazy with all six legs. Most of the time, they cling to underwater plants. In many ways, they look like they are trying to prctcnd they are not underwater at all—maybe they think they are like the leaf beetles on the willows by the shore. The diving beetles (pp. 124–26) keep their air supply under their wings, hidden from view, but the water scavengers keep air both under the wings and all along their undersides. Underwater, they look like they are coated with liquid mercury. To replenish the bubble, they don't just bob to the surface, either. Instead, they barely stick their head up, and let the air flow in around their antennae. For water scavengers, life is careful and slow. For diving beetles, it is risky and fast. There are 65 species of water scavenger beetles in Alberta. The biggest are the size of a Giant Diving Beetle (p. 126), but they are rare in Alberta. Smaller types abound, mind you, and the Obtuse Water Scavenger Beetle is our largest common species.

LENGTH: 15 mm.
RANGE: throughout Alberta.

DAMSELFLY LARVA

Order Odonata, Suborder Zygoptera

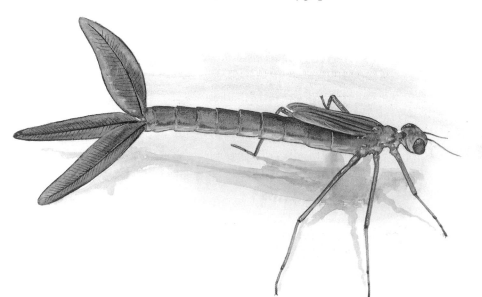

Here's an odd critter. At the back end of its long, slender body you see three things that look like dead leaves. These organs are the insect's gills, with which it takes oxygen from the water. Six long legs help it scramble among the underwater plants, where it watches for prey with its bulging compound eyes. When a small, edible insect is spotted, the larva takes aim and—"schnik!"—the folded lower lip shoots out, many times the length of the larva's head, and grabs the unlucky prey like the tongue of a chameleon lizard. Damselfly larvae are common in ponds and lakes, and they are easy to recognize. They are not good swimmers, mind you, and when they

LENGTH: up to 29 mm.
RANGE: throughout Alberta.

do have to swim, they wiggle through the water like a person with their hands at their sides. If you look closely at the top of a damselfly larva's thorax, you'll see four little wing pads. These pads will eventually become the adult damselfly's wings, when the larva finally climbs up out of the water and sheds its skin for the final time. There are 22 species of damselflies in Alberta, all of which have aquatic larvae.

DRAGONFLY LARVA
Order Odonata, Suborder Anisoptera

Damselfly larvae are weird, but dragonfly larvae are even weirder. Both have the folding lower lip that catches prey, and both have big eyes and slender legs, but there the similarities seem to end. Dragonfly larvae are bigger, heavier and more powerful than damselfly larvae. As well, instead of leaf-like gills, they keep their gills inside the end of their abdomen, in their rectum. That means, I'm afraid, that they breathe with their butt. And when they need to swim, what do they do? They squirt water out their back end, shooting through the pond with jet propulsion. The larvae of the darner dragonflies are long and streamlined, like the one shown here. Skimmer dragonfly larvae have longer legs and fatter bodies, sometimes with lots of spikes out the sides. Often, they become covered with algae and pond "guck." Perhaps the oddest dragonfly larvae are the snaketails, which spend their lives partly buried in mud at the bottom of streams and rivers and have smaller eyes and shorter legs. No matter what the species, dragonfly larvae take at least a few months to grow up, and when they emerge to become adults, they crawl up on plants or on the sandy banks of rivers. There are 46 species of dragonflies in Alberta, all of which have aquatic larvae.

LENGTH: up to 47 mm.
RANGE: throughout Alberta.

WATER TIGER

Dytiscus spp.

The Water Tiger is really just the larva of a Giant Diving Beetle (p. 126), and other sorts of diving beetles have similar larvae, too. Its name leads some people to confuse the diving beetles and the tiger beetles (p. 56), but tiger beetles only live on land, never in the water, at least in Alberta. A Water Tiger is a marvellous beast. It swims with all six legs in a very graceful fashion, floating almost effortlessly through the pond. On its broad, flat head the Water Tiger has eyes, but they are simple eyes, not the large, compound eyes of the adult. As well, the jaws of the Water Tiger are like two hypodermic needles, whereas an adult kills its prey by chewing on it with short but powerful jaws. The Water Tiger swims up to its prey and then attacks quickly and savagely. Once a fish or tadpole has been impaled, the Water Tiger injects digestive juices, and the prey dissolves in its own body. You might think such a feeding strategy would make Water Tigers some of the most fearsome

LENGTH: up to 60 mm.
RANGE: throughout Alberta.

creature in the pond, but they often fall prey to both Giant Water Bugs (p. 121) and the adults of their own species. Most Water Tigers prefer to eat small vertebrates, but some are more fond of eating insects instead. Like the adults, Water Tigers have to come to the surface to breathe. Their breathing hole is located right at the tip of their abdomen. There are nine species of Water Tigers in Alberta.

131

CADDISFLY LARVA

Order Trichoptera

To most people, adult caddisflies don't quite qualify as "cool" bugs. They are mothlike and only moderately colourful, and the only obvious things that set them apart from other bugs are their wispy, long antennae. But every caddisfly was once a larva, and caddisfly larvae are just plain nifty. Most caddisfly larvae are scavengers, but some eat algae, which they graze from rocks and water plants. While they are feeding, they are constantly at risk from all of the underwater predators around them, so most of them protect themselves with cases—coverings for their soft, grub-like bodies. Some larvae make the cases from twigs, while others use pebbles, reeds or leaves, held together with silk and saliva. Most cases are straight, but some are coiled like a snail shell. To find caddisfly larvae, look into a shallow pond and watch the bottom. Pretty soon, you'll see things move that you thought were just debris. These "things" are the larva cases. Trout eat many of these insects, by the way, and experiments have shown that they recognize caddisfly larvae by looking for their eyes. "If it has eyes, it must be alive" is the trout's rule, and, when you think of it, that's not a bad way to find bugs yourself. There are at least 200 species of caddisflies in Alberta.

LENGTH: with case, up to 60 mm.
RANGE: throughout Alberta.

SALMONFLY LARVA

Pteronarcys spp.

At first, the larva of a Salmonfly might look a lot like a great big young mayfly (p. 134) but look closely and notice the differences. Salmonflies are a type of stonefly (p. 107), and stoneflies form an insect order separate from the mayflies. A stonefly larva has only two long feelers on the end of its abdomen, where a mayfly usually has three. This feature is kept by the adult stoneflies, and, in fact, an adult stonefly looks a whole lot like a larva, except with wings. When the biggest of our stoneflies emerge as adults, fishermen call them Salmonflies (while entomologists call them Giant Stoneflies), and trout go wild trying to eat as many as possible while the feast lasts. Stoneflies don't live in ponds or lakes—they only like streams and rivers. Even then, they seem to prefer clear, fast-flowing water with lots of dissolved oxygen. Unlike mayfly larvae, which have gills on the sides of their abdomens, stonefly larva gills are tucked into their leg pits, so to speak. Without a powerful magnifying glass, and with an upside-down larva, they are tough to see. What do

LENGTH: up to 50 mm.
RANGE: throughout Alberta.

stonefly larvae eat? Mostly water plants and algae, much like caddisfly larvae (p. 132) and water scavenger beetles (p. 128), but some are predators. With their powerful legs, they hold on to underwater rocks and fight the current that threatens to sweep them away. There are 200 or more species of stoneflies in Alberta, very few of which are the size of a Salmonfly.

MAYFLY LARVA

Order Ephemeroptera

Some kinds of bugs seem to exist only for the sake of getting eaten by other creatures. Of course, this presumption isn't true, but it sure seems that way. Mayflies and their larvae are one such group, and they are about as defenceless as a bug can get. The 200 or so species of mayflies in this part of the world are either "crawlers," "burrowers" or "swimmers" as larvae. (The one pictured here [*Ephemerella* sp.] is a crawler.) Each type has its own style of feeding, and they all eat things like algae and detritus. Some even sieve food from the water with their hairy front feet. Some mayfly larvae live in streams, some in ponds, some in lakes and some in rivers. The easiest way to recognize them is by their three-pronged abdomen tip and by the fuzzy gills that line the sides of their abdomen. When mayflies emerge as adults, they generally live only a single day. At first they are called "duns" or "subimagos"—an odd stage that no other insect goes through. Then they shed their skin again, wings and all, and become the short-lived true adult, which lives only long enough to mate and lay eggs.

LENGTH: up to 30 mm.
RANGE: throughout Alberta.

SOW BUG

Oniscus aselus

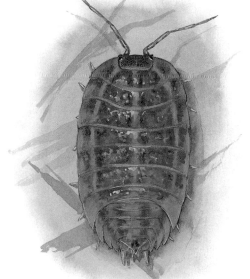

In general, insects are the bugs of the land and crustaceans are the bugs of the sea. Some crustaceans, however, do live on land (as well as in fresh water), although they need moist places to survive. Somewhere in the 1970s, we started noticing Sow Bugs in city gardens in Alberta, and they are becoming more common all the time. They were accidentally introduced from—where else?—Europe. It is interesting that European bugs generally do well when they are introduced to North America, but not the other way around. Sow Bugs are sometimes confused with Pill Bugs (*Porcellio scaber*), but we do not have Pill Bugs here. As well, Pill Bugs roll up into a ball when they are frightened, and Sow Bugs do not. They are all slow-moving, heavily armoured creatures that are easily recognized by their many legs and their many-segmented shell of a body. They are not harmful, and they feed only on decaying material, both plant and animal. Because our gardens are almost completely unnatural ecosystems to begin with, the addition of Sow Bugs is not much different from adding another species of non-native flowering plant. If, however, they spread into native habitats, I, for one, will be saddened by their presence—one more mouth to feed, messing up our Alberta-buggy heritage.

LENGTH: about 10 mm.
RANGE: unknown, but spreading, mainly in the cities.

GARDEN CENTIPEDE

Lithobius spp.

L ift a board or turn
the soil in your average
Alberta garden and you're likely to find
a centipede. The typical adult specimen is about 25
mm long and rusty orange in colour. Centipedes move
rapidly, twist like miniature snakes, and can squeeze into what seem
like the tiniest openings in order to escape, which is probably why you also
find them in basements so often. A slight opening between a window and the
foundation or a crack between wood and cement will allow them to get in.
Once in the house, however, they are no longer in contact with their most
cherished substance—moisture. They quickly dry out indoors, and when
you find them, they are usually dessicated and shrivelled to about half their
normal size. Centipedes are predators, and they have venomous fangs that
they use to subdue their prey. Our species are not dangerous to people, but
small children should still avoid han-
dling them. If you can get one to sit
still for a moment, you'll see that each
body segment carries one pair of

LENGTH: up to about 30 mm.
RANGE: throughout Alberta.

legs, and the legs are set off to the sides. (On a millipede, each segment bears
two legs, set underneath.) Despite their name, a 100-footed centipede is
actually an impossibility, because they always have an odd number of leg
pairs, giving either 98 (49 x 2) or 102 (51 x 2) legs in total. Centipedes can
have as few as 30 feet. There are about six species of centipedes in Alberta.

MILLIPEDES • NON-INSECT ARTHROPODS

GARDEN MILLIPEDE

Order Julida

The main similarity between a millipede and a centipede is that both their names end in "-pede," a word root that refers to their feet. Alberta millipedes are slow-moving, cylindrical animals that feed on plants or detritus. They have many more legs than a centipede, because there are two pairs of legs per segment, and each segment is shorter than a centipede's segments, as well. I suppose one could point out that a big millipede here is about the same length as a big centipede, but then so is a small worm or a matchstick. The great joy in finding a millipede is watching it walk. Because there are so many legs, they run the risk of getting in each other's way, so the millipede moves its legs in slow, coordinated waves, starting at the back of the body and moving toward the head. Speaking of which, the antennae on a millipede's head give this creature a somewhat insect-like appearance from the neck forward, and, indeed, the science of animal classification places millipedes closer to insects than centipedes. For those who know that millipede means "1000 foot" (centipede means "100 foot"), please make a note that millipedes always have fewer than 1000 feet. There are at least six species of millipedes in Alberta.

LENGTH: to about 30 mm.
RANGE: throughout Alberta.

NORTHERN SCORPION

Paruroctonus boreus

S corpions are desert creatures, right? So what are they doing in Alberta? Well, they do like warmth, so the only places you can find them here are on bare, sun-facing hillsides in the dry southeast corner of Alberta, from Dinosaur Provincial Park to the Montana border. The Northern Scorpion is, in fact, the most northerly species of scorpion in North America and the only one in Canada. Scorpions are unmistakable with their pincer claws, eight walking legs and long abdomen with a sting at the end. Some scorpions from much farther south can be deadly venomous, but the Northern Scorpion stings no more fiercely than a hornet. Mind you, reports of the effects of a Northern Scorpion sting are few, so it's best not to take chances. Even if you spend time in their habitat, you will probably have trouble finding scorpions—by day they stay under rocks. By night, however, they hunt on the ground for other small bugs, and it is then you can find them with a flashlight. If you have one, try putting "black light" bulbs in a portable fluorescent camping light. Under the rays of ultraviolet light, scorpions glow with an eerie green colour, making them much easier to spot. Remember, though, that these scorpions are rare animals here, so treat them with kindness and respect, and let them go back to their business.

LENGTH: 35 mm.
RANGE: only in the southeast corner of Alberta.

138

EREMOBATID CAMEL SPIDER

Eremobates docolora; Hemerotrecha sp.

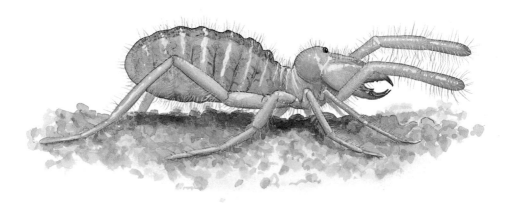

I t's unfair to describe these arachnids as psychopathic killers, but, hey, that's what they look like to most people who have encountered one. These oddball critters have a horrific combination of spiderish legs, a thin-walled, bulbous abdomen, a bit of hairiness and a front end that is made up almost entirely of jaw-like pincers. The pincers are held in an up-and-down fashion, rather than side-to-side like most other bugs, and they make camel spiders look horrifically mammal like when they chew. Their two beady eyes give no sense of intelligence whatsoever, and indeed camel spiders live mainly to kill other bugs. I suppose they also live to reproduce, and to their credit the mother camel spider guards her eggs for many weeks and stays with the young until they complete their first moult. Camel spiders can be found in the same sorts of hot, dry habitats as scorpions, and Medicine Hat is the camel spider capital of Alberta. These arachnids are also called "windscorpions," "solifuges" and "sunspiders." I prefer "camel spiders," the Arabian name, because we once had native camels in Alberta, and these bugs watched the rise and fall of the North American camel era, long before the arrival of human civilization. There are probably only two species in Alberta.

LENGTH: about 20 mm.
RANGE: the southeastern corner of Alberta.

HARVESTMAN

Phalangium opilio

I used to call these creatures "daddy long-legs," and as a kid I thought they were spiders. I now try to use the more traditional name "Harvestman" to refer to them, because just about any long-legged bug gets called a daddy long-legs. Harvestmen are not spiders, and unlike spiders, which have two main body parts, Harvestmen have no constriction between the head and the abdomen. Harvestmen are also unable to produce silk. Their eyes are set in a little mound on the top of the body, and their eight legs extend out from the sides. These critters are predatory, although, as you might imagine, they are no match for anything but very small prey. They will also scavenge on dead bugs or bits of decaying plants. Because Harvestmen are such familiar garden bugs, various odd beliefs have developed about them. Some people believe that they are extremely venomous, even though it is tough to get them to bite, which is, as far as I can determine, complete baloney. Another weird story has to do with the belief that if your cow goes missing, you pull off a Harvestman's leg and throw it on the ground, where it will point you in the right direction. There are at least eight Harvestman species in Alberta.

LENGTH: about 5 mm, without the legs.
RANGE: throughout Alberta.

ROCKY MOUNTAIN WOOD TICK

Dermacentor andersoni

Here's an unpopular "bug." To find one, take a walk in cattle country in late spring or early summer. Make sure to tramp through some long grass and some low shrubs, where ticks might be waiting to grab on to a passing "host." Then, before you go to sleep, take off your clothes and do a "tick check." Use a mirror for those tricky places. If you're lucky, the little things will still be walking around, looking for a place to plunge their mouthparts. If not, you have to pull them out, very slowly and carefully, with forceps near the head, because you don't want to leave the mouthparts in your skin. Most of the time, a tick bite is of no consequence, but they can carry Rocky Mountain spotted fever, and in the future they may carry Lyme disease here as well. An even more rare condition occurs when the tick bites at the base of the skull, and the unlucky victim develops "tick paralysis." Fortunately, all it takes to cure this problem is to pull out the tick. This species of tick is different from the Moose Ticks one sometimes finds or from the various ticks that pester pet reptiles in poorly kept pet stores. There are eight or more species of hard ticks (Ixodidae) in Alberta.

LENGTH: about 5 mm.
RANGE: most common in the prairies and southern foothills.

THIN-LEGGED WOLF SPIDER

Pardosa spp.

W olf Spiders are wandering hunters. Although they do not spin a web, they can still produce silk from the spinneret glands on their abdomen. Most of the time, you will see them in grassy places, where they search for other bugs. They are easy to find day or night, and if you search for them with a head lamp (not a flashlight), you'll see their eyes gleaming in the grass, like little points of dew. The trick is to go out looking on a dry night, when there is no dew to confuse you! Wolf Spiders have moderately good vision, and they can also see the patterns of polarized light in the sky, which helps them find their way around their grassy little worlds. Females are bigger than males, and when they lay eggs, they wrap them in a silk bag.

LENGTH: up to 10 mm.
RANGE: throughout Alberta.

The bag is then attached to the spinnerets, and the female spider carries the eggs with her until they hatch. These females look like even bigger spiders with blue or whitish abdomens—the blue or whitish part being, of course, the egg sac. When the young hatch, they cling to the body of the mother, holding on to special handle hairs on her back. There are at least 40 species of Wolf Spiders in Alberta.

BOREAL JUMPING SPIDER

Phidippus borealis

Even people with a deep-seated fear of spiders sometimes see a glimmer of cuteness in the jumping spiders. Sure, they have eight legs and eight eyes, but they don't move in the same creepy way that other spiders do. Instead, they walk around in a more insect-like fashion, if you know what I mean. They also jump. When you look at one up close, most of the time it will turn and look back, with a pair of big bright eyes on the front of its head. Jumping spiders have the best vision of any spider, and they can swivel their heads around to examine whatever catches their interest. Add to this the fact that some, like the Boreal Jumping Spider, have colourful bodies and iridescent fangs, and you have a spider with both a "face" and a personality. Many of the smaller jumping spiders also do complicated little courtship dances, waving their fangs, their palps (the little leggish things in front of the fangs) and their front legs like coloured flags. If the female likes the dance, they will mate. They are not aggressive, but the bite of the biggest ones (in the genus *Phidippus*) can be painful and unsightly. There are 50 species of jumping spiders in Alberta.

LENGTH: up to 10 mm.
RANGE: throughout Alberta.

ORB-WEAVER

Aranaeus spp.

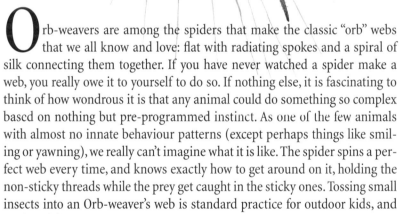

Orb-weavers are among the spiders that make the classic "orb" webs that we all know and love: flat with radiating spokes and a spiral of silk connecting them together. If you have never watched a spider make a web, you really owe it to yourself to do so. If nothing else, it is fascinating to think of how wondrous it is that any animal could do something so complex based on nothing but pre-programmed instinct. As one of the few animals with almost no innate behaviour patterns (except perhaps things like smiling or yawning), we really can't imagine what it is like. The spider spins a perfect web every time, and knows exactly how to get around on it, holding the non-sticky threads while the prey get caught in the sticky ones. Tossing small insects into an Orb-weaver's web is standard practice for outdoor kids, and we've all seen the spider wrap up its prey in silk and then deliver the death-fanging that injects the poison. These spiders also show us how easy it is for the average person to completely ignore an interesting sort of "bug"—only when they grow to full size do people notice them, and every entomologist gets phone calls every fall asking, "What IS this thing?" There are about 25 species of Orb-weavers in Alberta.

LENGTH: up to 11 mm.
RANGE: throughout Alberta.

LONG-JAWED ORB-WEAVER

Tetragnatha spp.

Oddly enough, in Alberta there are two families of spiders that make orb webs. One is made up of spiders that are plump and round, while the other is made up of spiders that are long and slender. The latter group is called the "Long-jawed Orb-weavers," and they are just as common as the regular Orb-weavers, especially in grassy areas. In mid-summer, a grassy field at dawn can be literally festooned with dewy webs, hanging heavy in the cool morning air. With their slender bodies, these spiders are harder to see when they sit in the middle of their snares, which they do much of the time. They also hold their front four legs together in front of the head and the hind four together behind the abdomen, to further break up their spiderish outline. Apart from their differences in body shape, the two groups of spiders have similar habits, and in both groups the males are smaller than the females and much more rarely seen. The family is named for the enlarged fangs, and when they mate the male and female hold each other by the jaws—probably the safest way to go about the matter. There are about 10 species of Long-jawed Orb-weavers in Alberta.

LENGTH: about 10–15 mm.
RANGE: throughout Alberta.

145

HOUSE SPIDER

Tegenaria spp.

Back in the good old days of damp, drafty basements, the only spiders you were likely to find in your house were the usual, secretive cobweb builders. Or, you might have seen Wolf Spiders (p. 142) that wandered in from outside and got trapped by the slippery sides of the sink or the bathtub (leading to the silly belief that they "come up through the drains"). Nowadays, things are a bit more exciting, thanks to two species of introduced house spiders from Europe. The most common is the Barn Funnel Weaver (*T. domestica*), which builds a sheet-like web in a dark corner of the basement. Then, there is the Giant House Spider (*T. gigantea*), which is, quite frankly, the creepiest bug in the whole darn province of Alberta. When a long-legged male goes running across the floor of the rumpus room, all eight legs flailing like mad, it is no wonder that most people call the exterminators. In B.C., one also finds the Hobo Spider (*T. agrestis*), which can cause an alarmingly ugly bite. (It is the only dangerous member of the group, if that's any consolation.)

LENGTH: up to 15 mm.
RANGE: centred on the major cities, but easily spread when people move.

BURROWING WOLF SPIDER

Geolycosa missouriensis

Every kid grows up seeing Wolf Spiders (p. 142) running in the grass—hunting spiders that don't spin webs and usually have a striped head. The biggest wolf spider in the province is rare, however, and it lives only in sandy places in the prairies. There, the Burrowing Wolf Spider digs its tunnels straight down into the ground, and lines them with silk. Waiting at the burrow entrance, these ferocious arachnids ambush passing prey. They are easiest to find when the weather is nice, just after a rain. When the sand is dry and hot, the spiders often close their burrows, and on open dunes the sand drifts across the top and hides them from view. Burrowing Wolf Spider babies cling to their mother's body using special hairs that are easy to grab, like handles for passengers on a moving bus. Burrowing Wolf Spiders use the same hunting strategy as the famous Trap-door Spiders, but the Trap-doors also make a silk-and-dirt "door" for their burrow. Since Trap-door Spiders are closely related to Tarantulas, some people (mostly school teachers, I'm sorry to say) think that the Burrowing Wolf Spider is a kind of tarantula that lives in Alberta. This assumption is not true, but this species is still a great spider.

LENGTH: up to 20 mm.
RANGE: only in the southeast corner of Alberta.

147

SIX-SPOTTED FISHING SPIDER

Dolomedes triton

If you read a lot of nature books, you'll eventually see pictures of these spiders eating small fish. They live in ponds and can walk on the water like a water strider, although they let their heavy bellies lay on the surface, because fully grown fishing spiders can't quite support their weight on tiptoes. They can also crawl around on underwater plants, breathing air trapped in the tiny hairs that cover their body and legs, so it is quite natural that they would eat small fish. I once worked in a lab where we studied these spiders, however, and none of the arachnologists I worked with ever saw one get a fish! They ate lots of water striders, damselflies and bugs that fell in the water, but no fish. So maybe it happens more often in other places, or maybe those photographs were posed. Female fishing spiders are bigger than the males, and they often eat the males during or after courtship. Females who have already mated are less patient with suitors, so males sometimes follow immature females, waiting for them to reach adulthood. When the female lays her eggs, she carries them in a silk bag in her jaws, unlike Wolf Spiders (p. 142), which carry them on their spinnerets. There are two species of fishing spiders in Alberta.

LENGTH: females to 15 mm; males to 10 mm.
RANGE: throughout Alberta.

WESTERN BLACK WIDOW

Latrodectus hesperus

Black Widows in Alberta!? Absolutely, but they are much easier to find on the prairies than elsewhere. The best way to see one is to walk around in mid-summer and shine a flashlight down old badger holes. Badgers dig way more holes than they need for their dens, so old badger holes are easy to find. The Western Black Widow spins a disorganized web, and it is just about the easiest spider in Alberta to identify: shiny black with a red hourglass on its tummy. The venom of these beasts can indeed be deadly, but fortunately they are shy and docile most of the time. Females do eat the males on occasion after mating, but this practice is actually fairly common among spiders, and it is not the macabre ritual that some people imagine. Apart from badger holes, the best place to look for Black Widows is in the grocery store, because many of them come in with fruits and vegetables. Sometimes they have red or orange markings on their backs, indicating they came from the southern states. And if you see a smaller spider with a smudgy orange-brown mark on its tummy, don't be fooled. It is the Boreal Cobweb Spider (*Steatoda borealis*).

LENGTH: females to 12 mm; males to 5 mm.
RANGE: prairies in the southeast corner of Alberta.

149

GOLDENROD CRAB SPIDER

Misumena vatia

H ere's the scenario: a big fat spider waits patiently in a fresh blossom. Sometimes the spider is yellow; sometimes it is white. Sometimes these colours blend in perfectly with the flowers; other times they don't. An insect comes to the flower for a sip of nectar, and suddenly it is spider fodder. My favourite story about this spider involved a butterfly, a Western Tailed Blue. The blue was flitting about in the greenery, stopping from time to time to sun itself, when it spied another blue. It flapped over to investigate, but the second butterfly seemed completely uninterested. That's when I saw the female Goldenrod Crab Spider, tucked up between the purple flowers of the vetch they were on. Before the first blue could comprehend the situation (if ever it could at all), the spider reached out, grabbed it, and had two blues for lunch instead of one. Not only had the spider used the flower as an ambush, it also used the first blue as a decoy! Males of this species are smaller than the females and are darker in colour. In a wild rose flower, they look almost exactly like the pollen-bearing stamens—the best buggy camouflage I know of in Alberta. There are around 30 species of "crab spiders" (Thomisidae) in Alberta, but not all sit in flowers.

LENGTH: females about 8 mm; males about 3 mm.
RANGE: throughout Alberta.

BOOKS FOR BUGSTERS

Unlike birds or mammals, there is no one book that covers the entire bug fauna of Alberta or any other state, province or country for that matter. You must be ready to face the fact that we possess a great deal of knowledge about a few selected groups of bugs and almost no knowledge of all the others.

It is sad that almost all the references that follow are out of print or hard to get hold of. This difficulty with references does not mean that the information in them is outdated. Names, both English and scientific, may change, and new information may be added, but for the most part these sorts of publications are as timeless as the bugs themselves.

The following books will take you a few steps further in your understanding of local bugs. I have avoided isolated papers in entomological journals, but if you are serious in your quest, the following references will quickly lead you to them as well. I should also mention two important series of books. The first is entitled *Insects and Arachnids of Canada*, and it was published by Agriculture Canada in Ottawa. It covers some of the spiders, beetles, two-winged flies and sucking bugs. Unfortunately, this series does not treat the entire Canadian fauna, and new volumes are no longer being produced. The second is *The Moths of America North of Mexico, Including Greenland*, and it is published by E. W. Classey Ltd. and R. B. D. Publications. It does not yet cover all of our moths, but the plan is to eventually treat each and every species.

You might also try searching the world wide web for information on specific sorts of bugs. As usual, some of it is well-researched and helpful, while most is not. Some groups, such as dragonflies, enjoy much better coverage on the web than others.

Books

Acorn, John. 1993. *Butterflies of Alberta*. Lone Pine Publishing. Edmonton.

———. in press. *Tiger Beetles of Alberta* [working title]. University of Alberta Press, Edmonton.

Arnett, Ross H., Jr. 1985. *American Insects: A Handbook of the Insects of America North of Mexico*. Van Nostrand Reinhold Co., New York.

Bartlett Wright, Amy. 1993. *Peterson First Guide to Caterpillars of North America*. Houghton Mifflin Co., Boston and New York.

Bird, C. D., G. J. Hilchie, N. G. Kondla, E. M. Pike and F. A. H. Sperling. 1995. *Alberta Butterflies*. The Provincial Museum of Alberta, Edmonton.

Bousquet, Yves, editor. 1991. *Checklist of Beetles of Canada and Alaska.* Agriculture Canada, Ottawa.

Cannings, Robert A., and Kathleen M. Stuart. 1977. *The Dragonflies of British Columbia.* British Columbia Provincial Museum, Handbook No. 35.

Chu, H. F., and Laurence K. Cutkomp. 1992. *How to Know the Immature Insects.* Pictured Key Nature Series. Wm. C. Brown Publishers, Dubuque.

Clifford, Hugh F. 1991. *Aquatic Invertebrates of Alberta.* University of Alberta Press, Edmonton.

Covell, Charles V. 1984. *A Field Guide to Moths: Eastern North America.* Peterson Field Guide Series. Houghton Mifflin Co., New York.

Danks, Hugh V., editor. 1978. *Canada and Its Insect Fauna.* Memoirs of the Entomological Society of Canada, No. 108.

Gordon, Robert. 1985. *The Coccinellidae (Coleoptera) of North America North of Mexico.* Journal of the New York Entomological Society, Volume 93, Number 1.

Holland, W. J. 1968. *The Moth Book.* Dover Publications Inc., New York.

Ives, W. G. H., and H. R. Wong. 1988. *Tree and Shrub Insects of the Prairie Provinces.* Canadian Forestry Service. Northern Forestry Centre, Edmonton.

Jaques, H. E. 1951. *How to Know the Beetles.* Wm. C. Brown Publishers. Dubuque, Iowa.

Kaston, B. J. 1978. *How to Know the Spiders.* Pictured Key Nature Series. Wm. C. Brown Publishers. Dubuque.

Layberry, Ross, Peter W. Hall and J. Donald Lafontaine. 1998. *The Butterflies of Canada.* University of Toronto Press, Toronto.

Lindroth, Carl H. 1961–69. *The Ground-beetles of Canada and Alaska.* Opuscula Entomologica Supplementa XX, XXIV, XXIX, XXXIII, XXXIV and XXXV.

Opler, Paul A., and Amy Bartlett Wright. 1999. *A Field Guide to Western Butterflies.* Peterson Field Guide Series. Houghton Mifflin Co., New York.

Otte, Daniel. 1981. *North American Grasshoppers.* Volume 1. Harvard University Press.

———. 1984. *North American Grasshoppers.* Volume 2. Harvard University Press.

Philip, Hugh, and Ernest Mengerson. 1989. *Insect Pests of the Prairies.* University of Alberta Press, Edmonton.

Pyle, Robert Michael. 1992. *Handbook for Butterfly Watchers*. Houghton Mifflin Co., Boston and New York.

Shaw, John. 1987. *John Shaw's Closeups in Nature: The Photographer's Guide to Techniques in the Field*. AMPHOTO, New York.

Wagner, David L., Valerie Giles, Richard C. Reardon and Michael L. McManus. *Caterpillars of Eastern Forests*. United States Department of Agriculture.

Walker, Edmund M. 1953. *The Odonata of Canada and Alaska*. Volume 1. The University of Toronto Press, Toronto.

———. 1958. *The Odonata of Canada and Alaska*. Volume 2. The University of Toronto Press, Toronto.

Walker, Edmund M., and Philip S. Corbet. 1975. *The Odonata of Canada and Alaska*. Volume 3. The University of Toronto Press, Toronto.

Westfall, Minter J., Jr., and Michael L. May. 1996. *Damselflies of North America*. Scientific Publishers, Gainesville.

Wheeler, George C., and Jeanette Wheeler. 1963. *The Ants of North Dakota*. University of North Dakota, Grand Forks.

White, Richard E. 1983. *A Field Guide to the Beetles of North America*. Peterson Field Guide Series. Houghton Mifflin Co., New York.

As well as the books, here is the contact information for various societies that can help you further your interest in bugs, and enhance your enjoyment of the subject. Some societies are local, and some are worldwide, but all have publications and meetings.

Societies

The Coleopterists' Society: Contact the society's treasurer, currently Terry Seeno, CDFA-PPD, 3294 Meadowview Road, Sacramento, California, 95832-1448. e-mail: <tseeno@ns.net.>.

Young Entomologists' Society: 1915 Peggy Place, Lansing, Michigan, 48910-2553. website: <http://insects.ummz.lsa.umich.edu/yes/yes.html>. e-mail: <YESbugs@aol.com>.

Entomological Society of Alberta: c/o Department of Biological Sciences, University of Alberta, Edmonton, Alberta, T6G 2E9.

Entomological Society of Canada: 1320 Carling Avenue, Ottawa, Ontario, K1Z 7K9. website: <http://www.biology.ualberta.ca/esc.hp/homepage.htm>.

Dragonfly Society of the Americas: c/o T. Donnelly, 2091 Partridge Lane, Binghamton, New York, 13903. website: <http://www.afn.org/~iori/dsaintro.html>.

North American Butterfly Association: 4 Delaware Road, Morristown, New Jersey, 07960. website: <http://www.naba.org>.

Lepidopterists' Society: c/o Los Angeles County Museum, 900 Exposition Boulevard, Los Angeles, California, 90007-4057. website: <http://www.furman.edu/~snyder/snyder/lep/>.

Other Resources

Provincial Museum of Alberta: 12845 102 Ave, Edmonton, AB T5N 0M6. Phone (780) 453 9100. Includes an excellent gallery called "The Bug Room," in which there is a representative collection of Alberta insects and related arthropods. You may also want to visit their website at <http://pma.edmonton.ab.ca/natural/insects/intro.htm>.

E. H. Strickland Entomological Museum: Room 218, Earth and Atmospheric Sciences Building, University of Alberta, Edmonton, AB T6G 2E9. A research collection of insects, with a website at <http://www.biology.ualberta.ca/uasm.html>.

And finally, for entomological supplies and/or books, contact:

Bio Quip Inc.: 17803 LaSalle Avenue, Gardena, California, 90248-3602. Phone (310) 324 0620, fax (310) 324 7931, e-mail: <bioquip @aol.com>.

INDEX

Page numbers in **boldface** type refer to the primary, illustrated accounts.

ABOUT THE ILLUSTRATOR

Ian Sheldon has been captivated by bugs since childhood. Born in Edmonton, Ian later lived in South Africa, England and Singapore. Exposure to nature from so many different places enhanced his desire to study bugs further, and he earned an award from the Zoological Society of London and a degree from Cambridge University. He recently completed a Master's degree in ecotourism development from the University of Alberta. Ian is an accomplished artist represented by galleries internationally, and he is both writer and illustrator of many other nature guides.

ABOUT THE
AUTHOR

As a child, John Acorn was hopelessly fascinated by insects—a benign afflic-
tion that eventually led to a Master's degree in Entomology from the University
of Alberta. His thesis work focused on tiger beetles, which are still among his
favourite insects. Today, he works as an award-winning freelance writer, speak-
er and broadcaster and is best known as "Acorn, The Nature Nut," host of an
international television series. John, a native Edmontonian, still lives in
Edmonton with his wife Dena and their son Jesse, where he spends most of his
spare time being exactly what you might expect—a bugster.